# Healing the Future

## Personal Recovery from Societal Wounding

DENNIS LINN
SHEILA FABRICANT LINN
MATTHEW LINN

PAULIST PRESS
New York / Mahwah, NJ

*Imprimi potest*
G. Thomas Krettek, SJ
Provincial, Wisconsin Province of the Society of Jesus

The Scripture quotations contained herein are from the New Revised Standard Version: Catholic Edition Copyright © 1989 and 1993, by the Division of Christian Education of the National Council of the Churches of Christ in the United States of America. Used by permission. All rights reserved.

The diagram "Magic Circle of Play" originally appeared in *Playing by Heart: The Vision and Practice of Belonging*, by O. Fred Donaldson, PhD., published by Health Communications, Copyright © 1993. Used with permission.

Cover design by Sheila & Dennis Linn and Stephanie Peller
Cover image: "The Lovers" by Marc Chagall. Copyright © 2011 Artists Rights Society (ARS), New York / ADAGP, Paris. Used with permission.



Library of Congress Cataloging-in-Publication Data

Linn, Dennis.
Healing the future : personal recovery from societal wounding / Dennis Linn, Sheila Fabricant Linn, Matthew Linn.
p. cm.
Includes bibliographical references (p. ).
ISBN 978-0-8091-4775-5 (alk. paper) — ISBN 978-1-61643-144-0
1. Christianity—Psychology. 2. Psychology, Religious. 3. Christianity and culture. 4. Christian life. 5. Conduct of life. I. Linn, Sheila Fabricant. II. Linn, Matthew. III. Title.
BR110.L57 2012
248.8`6—dc23

2011053217

Published by Paulist Press
997 Macarthur Boulevard
Mahwah, New Jersey 07430

www.paulistpress.com

Printed and bound in the
United States of America

# CONTENTS

For
Walter and June Wink
True friends,
Teachers of love and courage.


## Acknowledgments

We want to gratefully thank the following people for their help and loving care in the preparation of this manuscript: Michael Barca, Connie Barlow, Donna Crilly, Michael Dowd, Margaret Grant, David Ray Griffin, Pui Harvey, Walter Joseph Hanss, Jim Hug, SJ, Ken Jenkins, Julie Keith, Rich Lang, John Linn, Michael and Maria Morwood, Kristina Sadley, Steve Torma, Walter and June Wink.

## Introduction

# MUSICAL CHAIRS

> The future is an infinite succession of presents, and to live now as we think human beings should live, in defiance of all that is bad around us, is itself a marvelous victory.
>
> Howard Zinn[1]

We often begin our retreats by playing musical chairs. We set up six chairs in a circle and ask for seven volunteers. First we play the game the usual, competitive way. During each round, we remove a chair, and whoever is still standing must leave the game. Finally, only one chair is left, and whoever gets it first is the winner. Then we change the rules. This time we remove one chair during each round, but the remaining chairs can be shared. By the end of the game, the last chair has seven people piled upon it, laughing and holding on to one another so that no one falls off. Seven winners.[2]

We conclude by asking our volunteers about their experience. Typically they describe feelings of stress and anxiety during the first, competitive game. Then they tell us how much more they enjoyed the second way of playing and how relaxed and connected to one another they felt. The winner of the competitive version nearly always says that he or she enjoyed playing the second, cooperative way because "everybody won."

We experience ourselves as caught between two worlds. One is the world of winners and losers, as in the first version of musical chairs. This world is characterized by competition, rewards and punishments, individualism and domination. It's a world in crisis and full of fear. The other is a world in which the rules are changed so that everyone wins. This latter world is based on entirely different economic, political and spiritual assumptions.

## We All Have Dreams

Thirteen years ago, as we (Denny and Sheila) held our infant son, John, we dreamed of what he might do with his life. Now, when we read the newspaper headlines, we struggle to have hope for John and for his children.

During our years as John's parents, we have held on to our dreams for him and tried to heal our own wounds so we could be clear channels of love and support as he dreams for himself. How can we do this for the world he will live in as an adult? How can we stay healthy and open, so that instead of being overwhelmed by fear of the future, we are helping create the world of our dreams? How can we empower others to fulfill their dreams?

In our previous books we have tried to do this by focusing on familial/interpersonal wounding. Throughout the years of our ministry, we have searched out psychological systems and medical or scientific information that we believed would help our readers heal these wounds. Then we have integrated that information with prayer and Ignatian[a] spirituality, which emphasizes the divinity that pervades all things.

## A Toxic Womb

We did this integration, for example, as we (Denny and Sheila) awaited John's birth. We became aware of the profound influence of the prenatal period upon human development and

[a]This refers to St. Ignatius of Loyola (1491–1556), the founder of the Jesuit religious order and the author of *The Spiritual Exercises*, which is often used as the basis for retreats.

explored the field of prenatal psychology through our own healing process as well as in our research. Eventually we wrote *Healing Our Beginning.*[3]

In recent years, we have realized that, just as we are held in our biological mother's womb during the first months of our life, we are also held in the womb of the earth and its social and cultural environment. This shapes us profoundly. It now appears to us that much of the wounding we experience is at least as much societal and cultural as it is familial and interpersonal. Even during the prenatal period, the energy or tone of world events affects us, through the chemicals associated with our mother's emotional reactions that cross the placenta and enter our own bloodstream, as well as through more subtle energetic influences to which babies are susceptible.

Just as nicotine, alcohol or other harmful substances have a toxic effect upon babies in the womb, negative emotion and energy can create an emotionally toxic womb environment. A baby growing in such a womb is likely to feel overwhelmed by negativity, which leads to helplessness and hopelessness. Children tend to blame themselves, and rather than understanding that something is wrong with the womb, the baby may conclude, "Something is wrong with *me.*" We carry the effects of a toxic womb with us into adulthood.

The social and cultural environment in which we live is another kind of womb or energy field, and at this time in our history we perceive it as increasingly toxic. This toxicity can seep into our bloodstream, color our energy, cloud our existence and drive us into a trancelike state in which we can easily feel helpless and hopeless.

For example, our friend Julie just returned from four months of living with her family in small towns in the Caribbean and Europe. In those towns, what mattered most was connection to the human family across generations. For the first time in years, she experienced herself as living in a healthy "womb" rather than a toxic one. She describes how she and her family

> ...all relaxed into each other. We were very connected and moved as a unit, with a tremendous amount of laughter and enjoyment as we learned quickly that slow was better for us and less was a lot more.

When she returned home,

> I felt very out of sync, in my body and head for a few months...a definite mismatch between how and where my body and head wanted to move and what my obligations here required of me. As a result I was very agitated physically and emotionally, and easily annoyed. We had experienced a taste of our essential humanity, and it was beautiful to be so connected to each other and the community around us, both present and past. It felt so unnatural to come home and have those qualities not seem to matter at all. It wasn't as if we felt that our trip was a dream—rather, the "dream" was what we were living back home. I felt a great loss as the quality of our time away began to recede and I slowly returned to my life here. One could chalk it up to a "sabbatical vacation," but I am convinced it was so very much more than that...the quality of essential humanity in those small towns was so deep and felt so very old.

What can Julie do? If she went to a therapist (or a pastor), she might be treated for depression, encouraged to "adjust" to her environment, and so forth. However, as Walter Wink writes,

> All too often psychology is used simply to adjust people to an alienated and alienating society, with no recognition that clients' symptoms might in fact be a cry for deliverance from such a society. Patients are judged sick or well by the degree to which they are able to conform to general social standards of normality.... We behave like a species certifiably insane. Yet much of what passes as psychology and as religion simply sees it as its task to adjust people to *this* reality.[4]

## Societal Hurts

Instead of adjusting, how can we "live now as we think human beings should live"? This book is the result of a several-year journey in which we were nearly overwhelmed and paralyzed by the toxic and insane aspects of our society. During this time, our friend Jim said, "You look more scared than I've ever seen you. Notice what helps you. That is what you have always written about, and that will be your next book." We followed Jim's advice. As we noticed what helped us, we began giving retreats on "Healing the Future" to thousands of people in various countries. Our retreatants told us that they, too, had felt overwhelmed and paralyzed by our social environment. The material and processes in the following chapters are what helped us and our retreatants recover.

We used to publish a new book about once a year. This one has taken us five years to write, because it took us that long to "detoxify" ourselves sufficiently to gain perspective on what had happened to us. All our books are about healing, and include our own experiences of that. However, the hurts we were dealing with during the past few years differed from anything we had experienced before, and so this book differs from anything we have written before.

In our earlier books and in the retreats we have given in more than sixty countries, as we mentioned earlier, our focus has been on healing the hurts we experience in our families and other close relationships. We can speak about this anywhere in the world because we find that the deepest hurts are universal: lack of affirming love in childhood, unresolved grief for the loss of a loved one, sexual abuse and difficulty in forgiveness. Healing these hurts and related ones, as well as blocks to healing such as distorted religious teaching, have been the most common themes of our writing.

This book is different. Cellular biologist Bruce Lipton writes, "If you only focus on the person, you miss the influence of the field." By *field*, Lipton means the environment, which is ultimately nonvisible and energetic. He refers to Einstein's observation that "The field is the sole governing agency of the particle."[b] This is true at every level of life, from atoms to cells to human beings. Our families and other close relationships are aspects of the environment or field in which we were shaped, but those families and relationships are contained in and shaped by the larger field of our society.

Thus, our focus here is our social environment and how, despite its toxic aspects, we can stay healthy and open rather than being overwhelmed by fear and despair, so that we are helping

[b]Quantum physics reveals that despite the apparent solidity of matter, including the matter of our bodies, "...there is nothing other than energy. That means we are energy beings interacting with everything in the entire energy field...we are entangled in an unfathomable number of energy vibrations and we are connected to all of them" (Bruce Lipton, "How Your Beliefs Control Your Biology," July 3, 2008, http://www.brucelipton.com/articles/how-your-beliefs-control-your-biology/ [accessed September 4, 2010]).

Judy Cannato puts it this way, "A field can be described as a non-material region of influence that structures the energy of a system....Somehow a field holds energy and allows it to take form as matter...matter is energy bound within fields" (*Field of Compassion* [Notre Dame: Sorin, 2010], 29).

create the world of our dreams for ourselves and for our children. In other words, this book is about how societal hurts impact our personal lives. Certainly familial/interpersonal hurts and societal hurts interact and can exacerbate one another, as we will discuss later, but our focus here is on healing how we carry societal wounding. By "societal" we mean, first of all, American culture. However, the field of American culture now pervades our planet, leaving very few places untouched. The toxicity we perceive is increasingly global, and we hope what we have written will speak to readers beyond the United States.

We also hope that what we have written will speak to people of all faiths. Our first books were clearly meant for Christian readers. In our more recent ones, we have used increasingly inclusive language in order to reach the broadest possible audience, including those who have been hurt by traditional religion.

Each of us has religious images and constructs that we find meaningful and comforting. Here we have intentionally used the most universal images we could find (such as breath, light and spirit) for the sacred unity that holds all things together. Since we can only heal the future if we mirror that sacred unity by functioning as one family, this book is for anyone whose faith embraces everyone and everything.

## Humans Want to Care

Developmental psychologist Erik Erikson identified the stages of human development and named the gift of adulthood as *generativity*, meaning the capacity to care for others and to pass on life to the next generation.[5] Erikson's recognition of generativity is mirrored in the work of Marshall Rosenberg on nonviolent communication (see chapter 11). Rosenberg believes the deepest longing of all humans is to contribute to the well-being of others. In caring for them, we find our deepest joy and fulfillment.

Most of us will do anything to care for our children and grandchildren. When we hold them we often ache with longing to protect their future. Although that future may seem in jeopardy, it is not by accident that we are living now. Each one of us has unique gifts for caring that not only help us to carry out the special purpose of our own life, but also to contribute to the healing of the world we will leave to our children. As James O'Dea says, we are "evolution's best offering for this time."[6]

## Chapter 1

# REMEMBERING WHO WE ARE

How old are you?
Think of a friend. Is that friend older or younger than you?
Can you imagine what your friend looked like at birth?
Can you imagine how tiny he or she was at conception?

If you imagined someone older or younger than you, you are missing something. In fact, you were both born at the same moment, and you are both approximately 13.7 billion years old. At your birth, you and the entire universe were all smaller than a grain of sand. This was the moment of what is commonly referred to as the Big Bang, or what many call the "Great Radiance." You can see a baby picture of yourself, taken by the Wilkenson Microwave Anisotropy Probe, at http://map.gsfc. nasa.gov/media/101080/index.html. The picture is entitled "Seven Year Microwave Sky" and shows the oldest light in the universe. It's a picture of how you and the rest of the universe looked when you were only 380,000 years old. The globs of hydrogen in this image clumped together and eventually ignited into stars. With the exception of the hydrogen that was formed during the Great Radiance, the elements that comprise your body came from these stars. You are made of stardust.[1]

The original creative light from which the universe was born remains in everything. Science has confirmed the truth of this, with the discovery that every created thing contains photons that are the source of light and literally radiant. As the renowned quantum physicist David Bohm says, "All matter is frozen light."[2]

As a child I (Sheila) saw this light in all things. I don't mean I saw a physical light in the way I see the light from a lamp. Rather, I "saw" or sensed a vital, vibrating radiance or luminosity in everything. I took this so for granted that I did not even realize what I was seeing until it was temporarily gone, during an emotionally difficult year while I was in college. My greatest anguish was that everything around me—a table, a piece of paper, a dress—was now dead.

Our culture does not think of such objects as alive, but for me something living had gone out of all these things that had always been there before. Of course it was really I who had gone away, but I understood this only later. At the end of that year, as I came back to myself, gradually I saw the light in all things again. Having endured its absence, this radiant presence was even more evident to me and remains so. The "inanimate" objects around us are actually vibrating with radiance...the Great Radiance.

## We Come from Light and We Return to Light

Although the creation stories of many cultures have recognized this original light, ours is the first generation to have scientific evidence for it, and the first to even begin to understand the 13.7 billion-year story of how the light evolved into us. Similarly, we are the first generation to have researched near-death experiences (in which a person dies clinically and then returns to life), although humans have likely had near-death experiences throughout history. Current research "provides scientific evidence that the near-death phenomenon is an authentic experience that cannot be attributed to imagination, psychosis, or oxygen deprivation."[3] One of the most common elements reported by those who have had near-death experiences (NDEs) is a pervasive and infinitely loving light filling everything, including themselves. In an NDE, we experience ourselves as who we are: light. Just as light is our beginning, so also it is our ending.

Those who return from NDEs not only report seeing light, but deepening contact with their own inner light. This experience changes people profoundly. Regaining or deepening contact with one's light during a near-death experience can heal everything from fear and self-doubt to sociopathy and the long-term effects of trauma and abuse. Those who return from NDEs are able to give and receive love far more deeply and to know and carry out their special purpose in life.[4]

Because this light is our essence, it is always available to us, and we don't need to have a near-death experience to become aware of it. Each of us already has a way of perceiving it, although we may forget this because of unresolved hurts and the toxicity of our environment. Some of us see it as a radiance in the people and things around us, others of us respond more to the light of truth that we refer to as *enlightenment* and still others feel its tender warmth. Every movement of love is actually an expression of this light.

When we are in touch with our light, we live in a different space and we find different ways of being in the world, ways that are attuned to what is nourishing for ourselves and others. Conversely, when we change our habitual way of doing things to one that is more life-giving, we come more deeply in touch with our light.

For example, changing the way we play musical chairs is an experience of how powerful it can be to change the rules and do things in a way that allows us to live as human beings should live, so that everyone feels safe, empowered and loved. It reminds us that we are light and we can live from that light. When we are in touch with our light, we can change a whole lot more in our world than the rules for musical chairs.

## Healing Process: Getting in Touch with Our Light

1. Close your eyes, put your feet flat on the floor and breathe deeply. Place your hand on your heart and become aware that it pulsates with light, love and warmth. This is the light that formed you, is always within you and has guided you for 13.7 billion years on your journey from the Great Radiance,

   to becoming a star,
   to evolving into the earth and its elements,
   to being born just a few years ago to your human parents,
   and that guided you here today.
   Every heartbeat is this same light nudging you to take the next step in your evolution, in radiating the light you are.

2. Recall a moment from today, since you woke up this morning, when you felt most connected to that light within you and within all things around you. When today did you feel most connected to yourself, another, the mystery we call God, the natural world around you? Take a deep breath and allow the feeling of that moment to fill your heart again. Hold it in your heart and let it grow there.
3. Now look back over your life and see if a moment stands out when you experienced this same light and connection. Maybe it's being held on the lap of a person who especially loved you as a child, the day you were married or the birth of a child. Maybe it's a moment of healing or reconciliation, a special experience of nature, or a time when you shared your heart

with someone who really took you in. Maybe it's a time when you stood up for something you believed was right and felt deeply connected to your inner self.

Whatever it is, get in touch with that moment, hold it in your heart and let it grow there.

## Chapter 2

# POSITIVE MEMORIES: FIND THE ORANGE SHIRT

Our (Denny and Sheila's) son, John, has loved soccer since he began playing, just after he turned six. Although he's always played his heart out, during his first three seasons he scored only one goal, when he was on the orange team. As John looked forward to spring soccer, he had to confront his fear of having another goal-less season. When he got dressed for the first game of spring soccer, we noticed that his new yellow uniform seemed a little bulky. Then we saw his old orange jersey peeking out from under the new yellow jersey. We asked John why he was wearing the orange one. John said, "It's to remind me of the time I scored a goal."

John's strategy worked. That spring, he was the top scorer on his team. Instinctively, John knew that if he carried with him a reminder of the happiest moment of his soccer career—a moment when he felt connected to his own body, to his team members and to the whole universe on that beautiful fall day—it would help him overcome his fear of the coming season. John healed his fear of the future and empowered himself as a gifted soccer player through returning to a positive memory.

Moreover, as John healed his fear he expanded in many other ways. For example, although he was the highest scorer on his team, he didn't behave like the "star." He passed the ball to his teammates, shared turns for corner kicks, set others up for goals and cheered them on, made friends with members of the opposing teams...and generally held the whole soccer league in his large and generous heart. He liked it when his team won, but loved playing just as much when they lost.

## Positive Memories Change Us Physically and Emotionally

John instinctively understood the importance of returning to his happy memory of scoring a goal. Whenever we work with others, whether they wish to heal a hurt, make a decision or simply take the next step in their own growth, we begin by inviting them to get in touch with positive memories. We ask people to recall a moment when they gave and received love. Then we ask them to hold that memory in their hearts and return to it whenever they wish throughout their time with us.

Why do we do this? We learned it from St. Ignatius, who encouraged his followers to recall moments of what he called *consolation* and, whenever possible, do more of whatever gave them this consolation. Through the years of our ministry, we have come to understand why Ignatius emphasized this so much.

At the physiological level, memories of love bring our heart rate into coherence (a smoothly rolling, regular pattern), which in turn calms and strengthens us.[1] Positive memories may even alter our genes since "our perceptions of the environment, including our consciousness, actively control our genes."[2a] Moreover, recent studies of brain function have found that when a person recalls an

[a]Although genes do carry hereditary information, far less than 5 percent of us have defective genes that will cause disease. All the rest of us have genes that are quite capable of helping us live healthily. The emerging field of epigenetics is teaching us that these nondefective genes can be at least partially altered by the environment. Environmental signals are primarily responsible for activating chemical marks (the epigenome), attached to the genes and sometimes referred to as DNA referees. These marks turn off some genes and leave others turned on, in a manner somewhat comparable to a computer: the DNA is like the permanent hardware, and the chemical marks are like the software that directs the hardware. In other words, genes are turned on or off by chemical marks in response to environmental signals. This determines which genes will be expressed by an organism.

event in the past or imagines a situation in the future, the same regions of the brain are activated and in a similar pattern.[3] In other words, our ability to imagine a positive future is related neurologically to our ability to recall positive memories of the past.

Emotionally and spiritually, memories of love create a safe space in which we can face pain and uncertainty with hope and without becoming overwhelmed. When we remember that we have been loved in the past, we feel empowered to take the next step in our own growth and healing. We remember that the universe is fundamentally on our side and that we'll be given what we need. When we are in touch with what is right, it's easier to face what is wrong. Returning to positive memories is both a source of support in the moment, if the moment is difficult, and also a way of life that can help us create a new future.

## Positive Memories and Recovery from Addictions

Bill W., the cofounder of Alcoholic Anonymous and coauthor of the Twelve Steps, understood this. When he was twenty-two years old, he was socially awkward and depressed. In an effort to

---

Our perception of the environment is a critical aspect of how the environment affects the marks that turn our genes on or off. Thus, "Rather than being 'programmed' by our genes, our lives are controlled by our perceptions of life experiences." When we are in touch with positive memories of love, the genetic marks associated with love and safety are activated, thus turning on the genes related to health. When we are in touch with pain and stress, the "fight or flight" marks are activated, actually altering the DNA and predisposing us to illness. This begins in the womb, so that the genes of prenates are affected by their environment, including the extent to which their parents are in touch with memories of love. Bruce H. Lipton, *The Biology of Belief* (New York: Hay House, 2008), 20–21; Bruce H. Lipton, "Nature, Nurture and the Power of Love," *Journal of Prenatal and Perinatal Psychology and Health* 13:1 (Fall, 1998): 3–10; Bruce Lipton, *The Wisdom of Your Cells* (Boulder, CO: Sounds True, 2006), CD audio program; Amber Dance, "DNA Referees," *Los Angeles Times*, May 3, 2010; Mehmet Oz, "Flicking the Switch: The Phenomenal Circuit Board of the Epigenetic Frontier," Huffingtonpost.com, November 29, 2009, http://www.huffingtonpost.com/dr mehmet oz/flicking the switch the p_b_373026.html (accessed September 6, 2010).

join in at a social gathering, he took his first drink. Miraculously, it seemed to him, he became the life of the party. Reflecting on this later, he said something very important: "I felt that I belonged." Bill continued drinking, trying to get back that sense of belonging. By the age of thirty-nine, he was hospitalized for alcoholism and told that he would likely die of it.

Alone in his room one night, he cried out, "God, if you exist, help me!" Immediately, his room filled with light. A wind blew through him, "not of air but of spirit." He felt a presence, "a veritable sea of living spirit." After that experience, Bill said, "For the first time, I felt that I really belonged." He never took another drink.[4]

It seems that most, if not all, addictions and the compulsive habits we all have were in the beginning the best way that we knew how to belong—to ourselves, others and the entire universe. Bill's drinking was the best way he knew how to belong. The way out of an addiction or a compulsive habit is to find a better way to belong. Bill W. assures us that when we experience that sense of belonging, "all will be well with you here and hereafter"[5] and that we will change "automatically."[6]

Today, millions of people all over the world attend Twelve Step meetings. At these meetings, participants share what has diminished their sense of belonging since the last meeting and what has helped them recover it. Following Bill W., they know their recovery depends on staying in touch with positive memories of belonging and doing more of whatever helped them to experience that.[b]

---

[b]The principle of returning to positive memories can also be used to heal relationships. For example, Dr. John Gottman, who has studied marriage extensively, asks troubled couples to recall their first encounters and why they wanted to marry. If they are able to remember this with joy, they know a joyful relationship with one another is possible. If they know it's possible, they can recreate it. John Gottman, *The Seven Principles for Making Marriage Work* (New York: Three Rivers Press, 1999), 61–65.

## Rhubarb

If we (Denny and Sheila) were to return to a positive memory of belonging from this past year, we would think of rhubarb. When we were given the gift of our house in Vail at the time of our marriage, we planted rhubarb on a sunny hill above our backyard, where it's lived quite happily. Recently we found a new use for it. On Sundays in the summer, we buy our produce at the local farmer's market. We like the Miller Farms stand because they don't use pesticides. This past June, we brought them some fresh rhubarb from our hill and asked if they wanted to trade. They did, and for the rest of the summer we had all the fresh vegetables we could eat.

Miller Farms is located north of Denver. We learned that people can go there and pick food for a small fee of fifteen dollars per person between Labor Day and early November. After that, there is no charge. Last November, Miller Farms fed forty thousand people for free.[7]

So one day in October we went. The place looks like a cross between an old-time park and a farm. The rides and activities for kids near the entrance are free and low-tech—piles of hay, corn mazes, old tractors to climb on, etcetera. We got on a trailer attached to a tractor, along with a couple of other families, and the driver took us from one field to another—first the potato field, then carrots, beans, corn, peppers, squash, onions, cucumbers, cabbage…on and on.

Each time the tractor stopped, we all jumped off the trailer and ran through the fields, picking as much as we could. Everyone helped each other and shared. John quickly made friends with the other children, and they seemed about to burst with joy when we got to the corn fields and they started playing hide and seek. When we left, we took with us hundreds of pounds of fresh, healthy food. We gave a lot away to friends and neighbors, and still had more than enough for ourselves.

For those few hours in October, we lived in a world where there was enough for everyone—more than enough—and we all knew it. What moved us so wasn't just the abundance of food, but the abundance of care, generosity and happiness that rose up in each person in a place where we knew there was enough. We lived as human beings should live, knowing that we really do have everything we need.

Such experiences can remind us that there is another way to live, as when we play musical chairs. For example, our favorite restaurant in Denver is The SAME (So All May Eat) Café.[8] It's on a busy street in an area of the city where many homeless people live, often with little more to eat than cupcakes, chips and sodas from the 7-Eleven stores that seem to be on almost every corner. At The SAME Café, the food is fresh and organic. There are no menus and no prices. Customers choose what they want from a selection of soups, salads and healthy pizzas. Each person pays what he or she can afford. Those who cannot pay can work in exchange for their meal, washing dishes for an hour or helping with whatever else needs to be done.

The SAME Café has been a great success, and similar restaurants are opening in other parts of the United States. When we eat there, as on that day at Miller Farms, we feel ourselves in a healthy womb, free from the toxicity of our culture.

## Returning to Positive Memories

As John, Bill W. and Ignatius understood, when we find a positive memory that is especially meaningful to us, it's important to return to it as often as possible. For example, about two months after John's birth, I (Matt) was writing with Denny and Sheila in their home. They held John all the time when he was a baby, and I took over occasionally when they needed a break. If it was time for John's nap, he would sleep only when he was moving. I thought this meant I had to walk with him. So, I walked around and around the living room for three hours as I carried him. Whenever I tried to stop walking and sit down, John would wake up. I felt so much love for him that if he needed three days of walking without stopping, I would have walked for three days. Then I noticed that Sheila didn't walk around and around the living room with him because she had a secret: a rocking chair. I learned from Sheila how to rock John with the same movement as walking, and he kept sleeping.

Because he slept for three hours, I had plenty of time to give thanks for the special gift of John. One day as I felt my great love for him, I sensed this same love also surrounding me. My unconditional love for John was a revelation of the great, sustaining love that is within me and the entire universe. Now each time I need to remember this infinite love, I relive the love I felt when I held John. This is the easiest way for me to pray and often the most helpful.

Recently I was at twenty thousand feet staring out the window at an airplane's propeller. Suddenly the engine sputtered and then stopped. I panicked and feared this was my last moment as we began slowing down and losing altitude. But then I remembered holding John and, as I breathed deeply, I reexperienced the infinite love within me and all around me. With each breath, peace replaced the panic. After a few minutes, the engine started again.

I do the same prayer when I need to recover my creativity, for example, if I have to give a talk in an hour and still have nothing to say. I often hold a pillow to help me relive my experience of lovingly holding John and then let my awareness of this love grow with each breath. Within a few minutes I recover my creative life. But, then I have a new problem: deciding which of two good talks to give.

## Positive Memories of Play

As in Matt's story, we (Denny and Sheila) find that the most powerful positive memories are those we can return to often, especially in everyday ways. For example, a few years ago when we were especially troubled about the political situation in our country, we took our annual trip to Mexico to give retreats. It was a relief to be away from all the conflict and tension in the United States. We knew our challenge when we returned home would be holding on to hope in the midst of the atmosphere of anxiety we felt here.

Near the end of our trip, we gave a retreat in Zacatecas, a lovely mountain city in central Mexico. The retreat coordinators had arranged for us to stay in a convent, the home of Las Hermanas del Sagrado Corazon de Jesus y Nuestra Senora de Guadalupe (Sisters of the Sacred Heart of Jesus and Our Lady of Guadalupe). We expected the sisters to be as pious as their name, and so we told John, who had never stayed in a convent before, "Sisters like to pray a lot. You'll need to be kind of quiet. It's probably not ok to run around or yell while we're there."

The evening we arrived, the sisters welcomed us with a serenade and a delicious dinner. John noticed a volleyball court in back of the dining room and asked the sisters if they'd like to play. They told him it was too dark. In Spanish John said, "I saw some lights. You could turn them on." So John and the sisters left the dinner table, went out back and turned on the lights. Within a few minutes, those pious-looking sisters in their navy blue and white habits were running around the court, laughing and yelling at the top of their lungs. This same scene was repeated almost every night of our seven-day stay.

I (Sheila) was afraid to join in at first. I had played volleyball very rarely as a shy and nonathletic child, sadly aware that no team would want me because my tendency was always to duck rather than engage with any ball headed my way. I remembered an especially painful experience in sixth grade, during physical education class. Each child was asked to kick a ball. Unexpectedly, when my turn came I kicked it all the way across the field. Everyone cheered, and I received the most intense positive attention that I had ever felt from other children or teachers in the context of sports. For the first time, I felt hope that I could be a valued member of a team. They asked me to do it again. I couldn't. Now I was punished with equally intense disappointment. We all knew that any team I was on would have less chance of winning.

However, the sisters in Zacatecas didn't seem to care at all. They set up shots for me and both sides cheered no matter what I did. Eventually, I was running around the court, yelling as loud as John and the sisters, and feeling entirely happy and hopeful for the first time in months.

This simple story contains what we believe are the fundamental elements of healing fear of the future. Our whole family was playing—healthy, noncompetitive play without winners or losers. We lived fully in the present moment and were grateful for everything and everyone around us. We were surrounded by a loving community of people who accepted us exactly as we were. And, we were in touch with our own power, beginning with our feet that could run and our hands that could hit a ball.

After we returned home, we made an agreement with John to have "family fun" every day, as a way of going back to our memory of the love and healing we experienced in Zacatecas. We go out to play together even when our desk is covered with work waiting for us...especially when our desk is covered with work. Having fun, being together and using the power in our bodies restores us whenever we feel anxious or afraid.

## Healing Process: Finding a Positive Memory

We begin each prayer process with "breathing in and out," as a way to become aware of the spirit moving in, out and through us. In beginning with breathing and letting it remind us of how the spirit creates the universe through us, we are following an ancient Semitic custom. For example, in Aramaic, the word for *breath* and *spirit* is the same, *ruha*. *Ru* is the sound of inhalation and *ha* is the sound of exhalation. Ancient Aramaic speakers believed that each breath was a sensible manifestation of the one breath or spirit that created and continues to create the universe through them.[9c]

The Gaia hypothesis held by many quantum physicists is similar to the ancient Aramaic view. According to this hypothesis, "earth and all of its species constitute one living, breathing organism."[10] When we begin prayer with breathing, it helps us experience our vastness as we are entrained once again to the one breath that has moved through us, Gaia and the entire universe for 13.7 billion years. As Hildegard of Bingen said, "…prayer is nothing but inhaling and exhaling the one breath of the Universe."[11]

1. Close your eyes, put your feet flat on the floor and breathe deeply. Place your hand on your heart and imagine that you are breathing in and out through your heart. Recall that in Hebrew and Aramaic, the words for *breath* and *spirit* are the same, *ruach* or *ruha*. With each breath, be aware of the spirit's loving movement through you.
2. Bring to your heart a positive memory of a time when you were able to give and receive love. Hold that memory in your heart for a while and relive the parts that move you most. Let your feelings of gratitude and appreciation grow.
3. Ask yourself what aspects of this memory you might like to return to often in your everyday life.

---

[c]Thus, when Jesus used the word *ruha*, he was speaking about both breath and spirit. For example, the first beatitude (Matt 5:3), frequently translated as "Blessed are the poor in spirit," can also be translated as, "Ripe and attuned to the source are those who find their home in their breath" (Neil Douglas-Klotz, *Prayers of the Cosmos* [New York: HarperCollins, 1990], 47).

## Positive Memories Literally Change Our Hearts

If you had been hooked up to an electrocardiograph machine (a machine that shows your heart rate) while you were doing this process, your heart rate would probably look different now than when you began. This is because, according to research done by the Institute of HeartMath, getting in touch with a positive memory of love and holding your feeling of appreciation for it in your heart for even just a few seconds causes your heart to vibrate at a different frequency.[12] Your heart rhythm becomes more coherent (ordered, harmonious and efficient) rather than incoherent (random and jagged). This, in turn, affects every cell in your body.

Since the heart generates the body's most powerful electromagnetic field, it pulls or entrains the body's other energy fields into alignment with itself, including the energy field of the brain. (The electromagnetic field of the heart is about five thousand times more powerful than that of the brain.[13]) The brain is then less likely to focus on worry and stress and more likely to focus on love, empathy and creativity. In other words, loving feelings in the heart stimulate loving thoughts in the brain.[14]

Moreover, the heart's electromagnetic signal can be felt and measured from six to ten feet away. Thus, one person's heart rhythm affects the heart rhythm of other people who are nearby. So, if you hold your appreciation for a positive memory of love in your heart for even a few seconds, the increased coherence of your heart rhythm encourages the heart rhythms of those around you to become more coherent as well.[15] This simple process can bring healing or improvement in a wide variety of conditions, including congestive heart failure, diabetes, asthma, hypertension, anxiety, depression, attention deficit disorder (ADD) and hyperactivity (ADHD).[16]

When we learned about the HeartMath research, we reflected upon how much physical healing happens at our retreats.

We usually wait until the end of a retreat to include prayer for physical healing. By then, people have generally experienced a lot of emotional healing of the hurts that disconnect us from positive memories and block gratitude.

Consistent with HeartMath research, we find that physical healing happens automatically when retreatants are feeling grateful. As their heart rate becomes more coherent, this entrains or draws into sync other physiological systems, so that, for example, stress hormone levels go down, mental clarity increases, and the salivary immunoglobin A (the body's first immune defense) level and anti-aging DHEA hormone levels go up. Thus, the body is already moving in the direction of greater health.[17]

When we finally do pray for physical healing, we always begin by asking people to recall a memory of when they or another were healed physically. We encourage them to take in that life again, because by getting in touch with a positive memory, their gratitude and openness grows even greater.

It may be that when we are in touch with positive memories, we are connecting with the grateful consciousness that permeates the universe. That consciousness entrains our cells into the frequency of health that they once knew. Whatever the explanation, gratitude for positive memories seems to be a significant factor in physical healing.[d]

---

[d]Our focus here is on the role of gratitude for positive memories in physical healing. An environment of love and compassion seems to be equally important. In fact, positive memories and an environment of love seem to be mutually reinforcing and release the healing potential within all of us.

Note that healing is not a function of religious affiliation. Based upon his extensive survey of studies of the effectiveness of prayer, Dr. Larry Dossey writes, "As long as love, empathy and compassion are present, the prayer seems to work....I feel there is a great lesson in tolerance in these experiments in prayer. When it comes to prayer, no religion has a monopoly." From a letter by Dr. Larry Dossey to Dr. Martin Parmentier, December 3, 1994. Used with Dr. Dossey's permission.

# Chapter 3
# COMPETITION

The way we play musical chairs, or volleyball without keeping score, can help us remember our light. Playing cooperatively reminds us we are all brothers and sisters sharing the same womb from the first moment of the Great Radiance. Positive memories of moments when we lived in this way, without winners or losers, give us hope that we can live this way again in the future. They strengthen us in our ability to face whatever can separate us from our light. In this and the following chapters, we want to address some of the things that can separate us: competition, rewards and punishment, vengeful religion and living in a trance. We'll begin here with competition.

By *competition*, we mean that for me to win, you have to lose. If I get the last chair when the music stops, I win and everyone else loses. Our society assumes this is the only way to play, whether in sports, school, business, war or elsewhere. We are prepared to compete, beginning in early life.

I (Denny) remember many times when my grade school teacher called on another student and I hoped that child would give the wrong answer or make some other foolish mistake. That was because I had my hand raised and was waiting for the teacher to call on me so I could give the right answer. All through grade school and high school I competed to give the most right answers so I could get into the best college, where I planned to compete so that I could get the best job. A case could be made that the main subject taught and lesson learned in the classroom is competition.[1]

As soon as the bell sounded at the end of the school day, the competition continued with team sports. I never made any of the teams because I wasn't tall enough or fast enough or strong enough. Although competition made me a winner in the classroom, it made me a loser in sports.

In everyday life, competition is as pervasive as the air we breathe. The problem occurs when we just keep breathing the air and never ask, "Is the air so toxic that it can harm or even kill me?" The win/lose rules of the grade school classroom and playground become the rules for most economic and political transactions, as well as for war. However, is it possible to really win if it comes at the expense of others? Aren't we ultimately all in it together? We saw this clearly one day when John asked, "Who won the Battle of Lake Erie?" Not only had we never heard of the Battle of Lake Erie, but the deeper problem was that, even in a pacifist home like ours, in that moment John had forgotten that no one wins a war.

Our experiences of working in war-torn countries have made that all too evident. Among participants in retreats we have given for Contras and Sandinistas in Nicaragua, Protestants and Catholics in Northern Ireland, Blacks and Whites in South Africa, etcetera, everyone had lost peace, security and trust as well as loved ones. As we'll explore further in chapter 11, because of the commonality of loss, we lead such groups in sharing their stories and their grief so they can form bonds of compassion and work together for peace. Once bereaved parents realize that everyone loses children in war, they don't want it to happen to anyone else.

## Competition and Our Economic System

Competition, in which we lose sight of everything but winning, can make us oblivious to the death and destruction we cause, not only in war but in the promotion of an economic system that is leading to the destruction of all life on earth. Most of us have driven through a downtown area full of vacated buildings and then passed a newly constructed "big-box" store such as Wal-Mart, with a parking lot full of cars. Even as we write this book in the office that we added onto our house, we recall that most of the building materials were sold to us at cost by friends who owned a local lumber company for many years. Then, a big-box building-materials store moved in and our friends went out of business. The owners of the big-box company competed and won; our friends lost. But do we really need these stores that not only eliminate family businesses, but fill our homes with cheap goods—especially when 99 percent of the materials required to produce these goods end up in landfills within six months?[2] The resources required to make all this stuff and the toxins involved in producing it and disposing of it are destroying the earth's ecological balance. Liberation theologian Leonardo Boff describes the problematic situation of capitalism, which seeks competition:

> Capitalism is concerned with how to get more profit, seeking economic benefits by dominating nature, whereas ecology seeks means of producing and living in harmony with nature and with all beings. There is a fundamental incompatibility between them. Either capitalism renounces itself and thus creates a space for a sustainable form of living, or it will fatally take us to the destiny of the dinosaurs.[3]

It seems that win/lose competition has formed a template or worldview around which most of American life is organized, including our capitalist economic model. Unfortunately, as we travel to Mexico and other parts of the world, we see the big-box stores filling their landscapes, too.

Yet, Boff holds out hope:

> When, within a few years we reach the heart of the crisis and everything is at risk, then will be apparent the value of our ancestral wisdom and the origins of Christianity: "...in case of extreme necessity all becomes common." Capital, knowledge and wealth will be shared by all to save all.[4]

This may be hard to imagine if we have never lived in an environment based upon sharing rather than competition. Before we go on to explore further the dynamics and the implications of competition, perhaps it would be helpful to recall moments when we have caught a glimpse of Boff's vision.

## Sharing What We Have

We are the end result of 13.7 billion years in which cooperation has thrived over competition. Biologist Bruce Lipton writes,

> ...the biosphere is a structured cooperative venture comprised of all living organisms. Instead of invoking competition as a means of survival, the new view of nature is one driven by cooperation among species living in harmony with their physical environment.[5]

Hydrogen atoms combined to make helium. Molecules of helium joined together to form the stars. Stars generated sufficient heat to create the other elements that comprise the seventy-trillion-cell community we call the human body. Humans then joined together, beginning with small nomadic groups and ultimately forming the enormous associations that comprise modern cities. Despite the conflicts and competition so common in human groupings, everything we count on to sustain our daily lives would come to a standstill were it not for the basically cooperative nature of these groups.

For me (Matt) cooperation is an everyday experience. It's January and I came to Denny and Sheila's home in the mountains wearing the warmest jacket I've ever had. I got it from the "free table" in my Jesuit community, where anyone who has anything he doesn't need can leave it and whoever does need it can take it. A jacket isn't the only thing I received from the Jesuits. They gave me fifteen years of free university education. In our travels to over sixty countries, I have often stayed in Jesuit communities where I'm housed and fed for free. We welcome any Jesuit to stay in our house for free as well. When I receive a stipend for speaking or royalties for books, I send that money in to our Jesuit province office and it goes back out to whoever is most in need.

We have lay Jesuit volunteers all over the world who live in a similar way, as do the lay associates of many other religious orders. And this way of living isn't limited to religious orders or related groups. If there had been no jacket on the free table, I could have found one on line at www.freecycle.org. This is an internet-based organization with chapters in at least eighty-five countries and over seven million members. Anyone who has something to give away posts it on the site, and anyone who needs something posts that as well. Everything is given freely, with no exchange of money or other obligation. Estimates are that if what freecycle.org has saved from landfills in one year were loaded onto garbage trucks and the trucks were piled on top of each other, the pile of trucks would be five times the height of Mt. Everest. All this was accomplished by only one full-time staff person and some volunteers.

Another option for me might have been to wait until my summer writing time with Denny and Sheila. Every August for more than forty-five years, their local community has held one of the largest rummage sales in the world. Wealthy (and not-so-wealthy) families donate whatever they don't need to the "Minturn Garage Sale," which takes over the whole of a vacant local middle school building. Goods are sold at very low prices; an item of children's clothing might cost ten cents and a poor family could outfit their children for school for a few dollars. All of the profit (typically $120,000 or more) is donated to more than sixty local charities whose members volunteer to organize and staff the garage sale.

I (Denny) lived in the same way as Matt during my years as a Jesuit, and now Sheila, John and I try to base our life together and Sheila's and my ministry with Matt on values of sharing and cooperation. But if the Jesuits hadn't inspired us, probably millions of our neighbors would have. They are among the 26 percent of the adults (as of the year 2000) in the United States referred to by Paul H. Ray and Sherry Ruth Anderson as "cultural creatives." These are people who have made a "comprehensive shift in their world view, values, and way of life—their culture, in short."[6] These cultural creatives share:

> ...serious ecological and planetary perspectives, emphasis on relationships and women's point of view, commitment to spirituality and psychological development, disaffection with the large institutions of modern life, including both left and right in politics, and rejection of materialism and status display.[7]

Before 1960, only 6 percent of adult Americans would have held these views. In just a generation, a significant number of Americans have made shifts that in the past might have taken centuries. It caught even the most alert observers by surprise.

This change is not just an American story, but is happening all over the world, where groups based on values of cooperation, sustainability and care for the earth are springing up. According to Paul Hawken, author of *Blessed Unrest: How the Largest Movement in the World Came into Being and Why No One Saw It Coming*, there are currently one to two million such grassroots groups around the world:

> The dawn of the twenty-first century has witnessed two remarkable developments in our history: the appearance of systematic problems that are genuinely global in scope, and the growth of a worldwide movement that is determined to heal the wounds of the earth with the force of passion, dedication and collective intelligence and wisdom. Across the planet groups ranging from ad-hoc neighborhood associations to well-funded international organizations are confronting issues like the destruction of the environment, the abuses of free-market fundamentalism, social justice, and the loss of indigenous cultures....While they are mostly unrecognized by politicians and the media, they are bringing about what may one day be judged the single most profound transformation of human society.[8]

One example of such a group is Kiva (www.kiva.org), an international organization for *microlending*. This is a banking model developed by Muhammad Yunus, founder of Bangladesh's Grameen Bank and winner of the 2006 Nobel Peace Prize. Yunus pioneered lending small amounts of money to poor people who don't have the resources to provide collateral. In other words, he gives loans to the people who usually can't get them but most need them. The rate of loan defaults is astoundingly low; 98.57 percent of loans from the Grameen Bank have been repaid on time, a much higher rate than would be found at any typical commercial bank.[9]

Kiva extends the principle of microlending to anyone who wants to participate. People who need loans and people who want to extend them are matched through the internet. Kiva loans are interest free and are usually limited to $25, small enough that children can participate in giving a loan.[10] Our John has given four Kiva loans thus far, all to people in Latin America who have small businesses related to food. He chose these recipients because he hopes to meet them during one of our trips to Latin America, where we often work. Also, John figures food is what people most need to survive.

John shared his enthusiasm for giving Kiva loans with our neighbor, Steve, whose work is buying and selling businesses. Steve was so moved by this different model of entrepreneurship that he currently has fifty loans in his Kiva portfolio.

The power of Kiva and the one to two million other such groups comes from two shared principles: the Golden Rule and the sacredness of all life. These are the basic principles of the world's major religions.[11] People who adhere to these principles are in effect, the immune defense system of our planet. Because our culture tends to frame things competitively and to use metaphors from sports and war,

> ...when we hear the word *defense*, we think *attack*, but the defense of the world can truly be accomplished only by cooperation and compassion....According to immunologist Gerald Callahan, "faith and love are literally buried in our genes and lymphocytes, and what it takes to arrest our descent into chaos is one person after another remembering who and where they really are."[12]

## Healing Process: Memories of Cooperation

Perhaps realizing that we are part of a vast movement in the direction of cooperation, in which everyone wins, can sustain us as we explore competition further. We suggest the following process:

1. Sit comfortably, close your eyes and place your hand on your heart. Let your awareness go down into your heart and imagine that you are breathing in and out through your heart.
2. Recall an example of cooperation and sharing that you have experienced. Perhaps you will think of a volunteer organization, a time when you reached out to a needy person or someone reached out to you when you were needy, a story of compassion in another part of the world that moved you deeply, etcetera.
3. Recall how you felt about this experience. Hold your feelings in your heart and let them grow there.
4. Let yourself imagine a world in which such experiences were commonplace and even the norm.
5. Continue to breathe deeply as you hold that image and the feelings it evokes in your heart, letting them grow within you.

## Competition and Play

Although competition is pervasive in American life, we want to focus on play because how we play affects how we live. Perhaps if we could imagine ourselves playing differently, we could begin to imagine ourselves living differently. Most people play through games and sports, and most games and sports involve competition. Wherever we travel, competitive sports seem to be the most watched and the most glorified events of daily life. Criticizing this may provoke quite a reaction; good friends we have discussed it with have all but blown up at us. So, let's begin with the healthy and life-affirming aspects of sports.

For most of us, games and sports are a way to have fun while building relationships, enjoying nature, improving our skills, overcoming obstacles and exercising our minds and/or our bodies. I (Denny) experienced this during one of the most rewarding sports experiences of my life. Although I never considered myself a good athlete, forty years ago I decided to set what seemed an impossible goal: to run fifty miles in one day. Two friends who were runners said they would help me train for three months and then run along with me. Three other friends offered to be a support crew on bicycles, bringing me water and honey for energy. When I finally crossed the finish line, my friends were as excited as I was. My memory of that day and of feeling connected to myself, my friends and the earth is such a happy one that I have continued jogging three or four times a week ever since. Those jogs are a constant reminder to me that no goal is impossible.

Someday I would like to run in the world's longest certified foot race, the "Self Transcendence Race," held each year in a neighborhood in New York City. The route covers the perimeter of just one city block. During a two-month period from mid-June to mid-August, runners have the opportunity to discover their limits and capacities and go beyond themselves. There is no stadium, no medals, no multimillion-dollar contracts and no sponsorships. Runners such as Suprabha Beckjord (who completed 3,100 miles in 58 days, 7 hours, 54 minutes and 27 seconds) are encouraged by their fellow runners and also greeted by neighbors and students who make daily visits to the race and provide homemade meals and snacks. Such races help runners (and the entire neighborhood) "discover the limits of their capacities."[13]

## Competition Makes Us Sick

Coaching my son's soccer team has been very different from my cooperative experience of running. A few years ago, John was a member of the Golden Eagles. During their game with the Red Dragons, I heard one of our players, Andy, shouting to his teammates, "Kill him! Kill number 16! Kill him…!" I asked Andy, "Why do you want to kill him?" Andy said, "Because every one of those Red Dragons is our enemy." What frightened me is that he seemed to believe what he was saying. But I didn't have time to finish my conversation with Andy because seconds later number 16 lay injured on the field. Like someone suddenly coming out of a trance, Andy stopped the conversation and rushed onto the field to help carry number 16 to the sidelines. As it turned out, Andy and number 16 (Gus) were lifelong friends. I was left wondering how a game of soccer can put someone into such a state that he sees his closest friend as an enemy he wants to kill.

It seems that Andy is one of the lucky ones. Somehow the injury of Gus helped Andy remember that friendship matters more than winning. For many athletes, sports competition causes corrosion of otherwise close friendships. According to psychotherapist Lillian Rubin, this is because values of win/lose competition, such as trying to demonstrate invincibility during a game, are the opposite of those that would make one vulnerable and open to the emotional support that deep friendships require.[14] Studies suggest that the way we play on the field is probably the way we will play out our lives. Thus, among successful athletes, "characteristics such as kindness, sympathy, and unselfishness are notably absent." A personality profile of fifteen thousand athletes showed "a low interest in receiving support and concern from others, a low need to take care of others, and a low need for affiliation." Researchers concluded that such a personality "seems necessary to achieve victory over others."[15]

In other words, loving connection and competition appear to be antithetical. As O. Fred Donaldson writes,

> Contest is a centrifugal force, scattering and atomizing people as groups and individuals whose self-awareness depends on identifying others as outsiders. The foundation of contest relationships is that in order to experience oneself as a winner one has to suppress one's awareness of the need for losers. Those

> who lose know of no other way of relating than to adopt the methods of the winners and create other losers. Our self-esteem is built upon the quicksand of lowering the esteem of others.[16]

Evidence that competitive sports can be hurtful to relationships may come as a surprise, especially to those who hold the *catharsis theory*. This is the theory that watching or playing a competitive sport is a healthy way of *catharting*, or draining off, aggression. According to Alfie Kohn, author of *No Contest: The Case Against Competition*, who has reviewed studies of this theory, "few beliefs so widely held by the general public have been so decisively refuted by the evidence."[17] In fact,

> Watching others be aggressive does not discharge our own aggressiveness. What seems to happen instead is straightforward modeling: we learn to be aggressive. Our restraints against aggression are lowered...one study after another has failed to show any catharsis effect.[18]

As for athletes themselves, over the course of a season they were found to become *more* aggressive, according to personality tests. This was true of high school football players as well.[19]

This correlation between sports and aggression holds true for entire societies. For example, cross-cultural studies confirm that the more a nation participates in highly competitive sports that simulate or involve actual combat (e.g., football, hunting, boxing), the more warlike that nation is. Conversely, cultures that avoid war have a low level of combative sports. Combative sports and war would be inversely related if the catharsis theory were true. However, they are directly related.[20]

## Sports and War

Since the ultimate of wishing failure on another is war, in which we seek to totally "beat" or annihilate another, it may not surprise us that the more aggressively competitive a sport is, the more the language and action of that sport resemble war. Consider the Super Bowl, which is a composite of patriotism (singing the national anthem, waving the flag, etc.), corporate marketing (a thirty-second advertisement costs 2.1 million dollars) and competition. It is usually the single most watched event in the world. What does the Super Bowl tell viewers about America? Following is a description of the purpose of football, by comedian George Carlin:

> In football, the object is for the quarterback, otherwise known as the field general, to be on target with his aerial assault, riddling the defense by hitting receivers with deadly accuracy in spite of the blitz, even if he has to use the shotgun. With short bullet passes and long bombs, he marches his troops into enemy territory, balancing his aerial assault with a sustained ground attack, which punches holes in the forward wall of the enemy defensive line.[21]

This warlike language is used to describe not only the Super Bowl but also "sandlot" football games that, as children, our athlete friend and his buddies called, "Run-Tackle, Kill-Smear."

The January 26, 2003, Super Bowl, between the Oakland Raiders and Tampa Bay Buccaneers, illustrated dramatically the way that sports carry over into life. That day Oakland lost more than the game (48 to 21), as riots broke out on their streets. Twelve cars were set on fire, and a McDonald's almost burnt down. Four hundred police officers could not contain the rioters chanting, "Raiders rule, f— the police."

If you missed the Super Bowl and the Oakland riots, never mind, because shortly afterward there was a rerun. America was still on display for the world to see, but a few names had changed. This time it was not the Oakland Raiders versus the Tampa Bay Buccaneers, but America versus Iraq. No longer was it four hundred Oakland police trying to contain the Oakland Raider fans. Rather, it was the United Nations and most of the world trying to contain the Americans from raiding Iraq and setting it on fire. It was March 19, 2003, and to most Americans it was known as Operation Iraqi Liberation (OIL). But to much of the rest of the world, it would become known as the American raid on Iraqi oil.

Although Oakland Raider quarterback Rich Gannon was replaced by American Field General Tommy Franks, the play-by-play action displayed on worldwide television was basically the same as the football attack described above. America was on target with its aerial assault of cruise missiles, riddling Iraqi defenses by bombing them with deadly accuracy. As Baghdad was bombed, General Franks marched American troops into Iraqi enemy territory, thus balancing the American aerial assault with a sustained ground attack.

Could it be that, just as studies of the catharsis theory suggest, our American preoccupation with highly competitive sports like football has numbed us to violence? Watch a war on TV and pretend it's a football game. No body bags will be shown. Perhaps President Dwight D. Eisenhower anticipated this when he said, "The true mission of sports is to prepare young people for war."[22]

## Is Healthy Competition a Contradiction in Terms?

That same day that Andy recognized injured Red Dragon number 16 as his friend, Gus, rather than as an enemy, I had to face what competition does to me. With only a few minutes left to play, the game was tied. Number 16 lined up to kick a penalty shot, and my son, as goalie, prepared to block it. Silently I was screaming at number 16, "Miss it!" I wanted him to fail. Apparently number 16 wasn't listening, because his perfectly aimed kick passed safely through the corner of the soccer goal so quickly that my lunging son didn't have a chance. To make matters worse, I had to applaud number16 because the rules in my son's league required parents, if they wanted to cheer at all, to cheer for players on both teams.

As I struggled to applaud number 16, I knew that my heart had been like Andy's. Neither Andy nor I wanted number 16 to succeed. We both wanted him to fail so his side would lose and our side would win. I had to decide whether I really want to live in a world of friends and enemies, good guys and bad guys, wishing success to some and failure on others. I don't.

Probably most of us playing sports would say that we are seldom aware, as I was that day, of wishing failure on anyone. When we are in the trance of competition, our focus is only on winning, and we try to make our opponent fail by missing the goal, striking out or otherwise making the wrong move. That we are only aware of wanting to win does not excuse us, any more than the big-box lumberyard can be excused for not thinking of the consequences that building their lumberyard might have on my friend's family business. Unfortunately, the door of the locker room opens directly to the door of the corporate board room.

Although competitive sports can help achieve honorable goals, such as building character through teamwork, perseverance, etcetera, at what expense? Is it worth it when what makes us winners on the playing field can make us losers at life? Are there more cooperative ways of playing that would achieve those same honorable goals without the harmful side effects?

## Competition Versus Cooperation

In our discussions with friends about sports, they understand the extremes to which sports can lead, such as the Oakland riots following the Super Bowl. But some wonder if we're going too far. They say, "What about a friendly round of golf? Playing against someone else helps me improve my skills." Or, "When I play tennis with my friends, we forget who won ten minutes after the game is over. We just like being together." Isn't competition under these circumstances harmless?

A helpful analogy might be the children's TV program, *Sesame Street*. The content seems harmless, even positive in some ways. But, as Marshall McLuhan said, "The medium is the message." In other words, the medium of television affects the developing brains of children regardless of the seemingly harmless content of a program like *Sesame Street*. And the effects of television on young children are not positive. They include so many academic, social and health problems that many experts on early childhood development are now advising that children should not watch television (nor computer screens) before the age of five.[23]

Perhaps the medium is also the message with competition. Even though it may be fun, friendly, help us develop skills and so forth, the fundamental dynamic is that in order for me to win I have to try to make you lose or at least hope you fail in some way. Could it be that any competitive play reinforces a worldview that is destroying life on our planet? Could it be that any cooperative play strengthens an alternative worldview that will make life more enjoyable and sustainable? What we mean is that, regardless of whether we are playing golf or football, Chinese checkers or Scrabble, certain unavoidable aspects of competition are involved that will color our way of being in the world. Although we can try to minimize the negative aspects of competition (for example, by forgetting about the score ten minutes after the game is over), the very fact that we are choosing to participate in an activity based upon winners and losers reinforces a destructive way of life.

We can summarize the difference between the extremes of competition and cooperation as follows:

| **Competition** | **Cooperation** |
|---|---|
| 1. I learn that to have fun means I have to win and you have to lose. As Vince Lombardi said, "Winning isn't everything; it is the only thing." | 1. Fun means making sure that we both win. We are all one, and when you win, I win too. When you lose, I lose too. |
| 2. I feel happy when you fail (or I make you fail) or when I prove myself better than you. | 2. I want your success as much as I want my own. Therefore I am delighted when you make a great play. |
| 3. Developing my skill is what counts. | 3. Helping each other develop our skills is what counts. |
| 4. Relationship might grow in spite of the competition. | 4. Relationship grows because I want the best for you. |

## Sharing the Ultimate Yeast Energy Drink

The idea that competition is inherently destructive may be quite hard to grasp, since sports may be our primary way of having fun, socializing and exercising, and we may not be able to imagine any other way to play. We (Denny and Sheila) experience this with our son, John. He loves soccer, and being on a team is one of his main ways of socializing with other children and experiencing other adults as teachers (both values for us, since John is home-schooled). We don't want to take John out of his soccer program and, although we've had tentative conversations with his coaches, we don't sense any movement yet toward revamping the game to eliminate competition. It seems the best we can do for now is model cooperative attitudes for him (applauding the other team as well as his) and encourage his own cooperative instincts (such as the time his team was playing a team with several wounded players and John offered to go over and play for that side instead of for his own).

Meanwhile, we want to minimize competition and maximize cooperation in sports and games whenever we can. Years ago, when we (Denny and Matt) worked on the Sioux Indian Reservation, we learned how this can be done from the track coach, Gene Loverich. Because our school on the reservation was so small, we never won any track meets. This changed when Gene arrived. He was an engineer who used his scientific training to make himself into an accomplished marathon runner. He brought his many notebooks filled with charts that analyzed every facet of running. He had documented the effects of everything from physical workouts to diet to imagination exercises. Unfortunately the "ultimate yeast energy drink" he concocted had to be consumed before, during and after each cross-country meet...if it didn't kill you the first time.

A few months later, Gene's runners handily won the state championship. They continued to win for most of the years that Gene coached. If ever there was a year that our team didn't win, it was because Gene gave out his notebooks with all their "secrets" to any coach from another team that asked. He showed the same care for their runners as for his own. Sometimes at a cross-country meet we would see him cheering for one of the opposition runners. He wanted every student to do well, on his team and on all the other teams. He was doing what he could to change athletic competition into athletic cooperation. Gene understood that we really only win when everyone else wins, too.

Like ourselves, many readers may have experienced something similar at family reunions with their baseball games. At our summer reunion game last year, some adults as well as younger children were given not just three but four or five strikes when they needed it. And, if someone was fortunate enough to hit the ball but didn't quite make it to first base on time, it didn't matter. He or she was still declared "safe." It seemed there were no "outs," even when there was an out. No one cared about the score. We all just wanted to help each other have the most fun possible. Since childhood, baseball games have been the high point of our (Denny and Matt's) family reunions. Even though we are playing a sport, when we don't wish failure on anyone and when everyone wins, we are in the realm of cooperation rather than competition. We have left what O. Fred Donaldson calls "cultural play" and entered "the magic circle of play":[24]

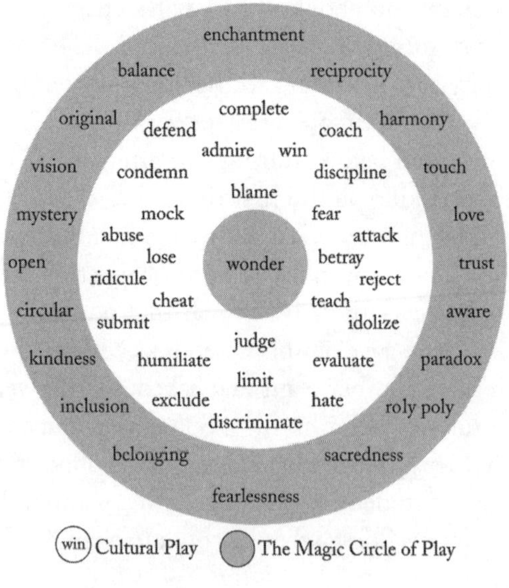

Perhaps we can stay in the magic circle of play and begin to eliminate competition entirely from sports and games. A number of creative people have proposed ways of doing this. For example, Terry Orlick has found noncompetitive ways to play hundreds of games, including everything from Scrabble to volleyball. We learned our way of playing musical chairs from him.[25]

We're going to try Orlick's suggestion for volleyball the next time we go to Zacatecas. In "bump and scoot volleyball," every time a player bumps the ball over the net, he or she then scoots to the other side. The shared objective of all the players is to make a complete change of teams with as few drops of the ball as possible.[26] We believe that the more a sport helps us to experience ourselves as part of a family, wishing the best for everyone, the healthier that sport and the healthier our world.

Are we dreaming impossible dreams, far removed from the "real world"? We don't think so, because the "real world" isn't real, isn't working and won't last. Paul Hawken expresses this as follows:

> There are two kinds of games—games that end and games that don't. In the first game, the rules are fixed and rigid. In the second, the rules change whenever necessary to keep the game going. James Carse called these, respectively, finite and infinite games. We play finite games to compete and win. They always have losers and are called business, banking, war, NBA, Wall Street, and politics. We play infinite games to play; they have no losers because the object of the game is to keep playing. Infinite games pay it forward and fill future coffers. They are called potluck, family, samba, prayer, culture, tree planting, storytelling, and gospel singing. Sustainability, ensuring the future on earth, is an infinite game, the endless expression of generosity on behalf of all.[27]

## Postscript: We Don't Have the Answer

Competition is a complex issue that continually challenges us as we (Denny and Sheila) try to raise a cooperative child in a competitive culture, where so much of John's sense of belonging to a community of peers comes through sports. As with soccer, each sport John participates in confronts us with this dilemma once again. For example, this year's Christmas letter was written during basketball season and begins as follows:

Dear Friends,

We want to tell you two stories about dreams. One came true and the other will some day.

The first story is about our John. Although we're still home schooling, last year John was welcomed into the sports program of Vail Mountain School, a private school near our home. Most afternoons, he's with a group of good friends and superb coaches for soccer, basketball, ski racing or track and field, depending on the time of year. We're very grateful to VMS for including John, and he has a special desire to be a valued member of his team.

When basketball began this fall, John was having difficulty making baskets. He practiced endlessly at the hoop in our driveway, but still he went into the first game feeling unsure of himself. Near the end of the fourth quarter, VMS was losing 13 to 12. John had been in and out of the game and now he was on the bench. With nine seconds left, the coach put him back in. With three seconds left, John's team had the ball. The coach called for a time out and said to the boys, "We can do this." John told us later, "I believed him." Coach instructed Nick to throw the ball to John from the sideline and John was to shoot. John caught the ball from Nick, pivoted and, without a moment to plan his shot, he let it go. The ball left his hands just before the buzzer went off…and went in. The whole gym exploded, cheering for John. His teammates nearly crushed him with hugs. Just like in a movie.

Denny turned to Sheila with tears in his eyes and said, "All day I saw John make the winning basket at the end of the game. When he was on the bench nine seconds before the end, I didn't know how it could still happen. But I saw it all day." Denny's dream for John, and John's dream for himself, came true. On the way home, John said, "I have to give some of the credit to Nick. He got the ball to me."

[The letter goes on with another story about a dream.]

We realize that our letter seems to contradict much of this chapter. And yet, we have to admit that the "impossible basket," as our family now calls it, was the highlight of John's year. It's a positive memory he will return to all his life whenever he wants to accomplish something against great odds.

Was there another way in which John could have achieved the same thing, without competition? We don't have the answer and can only say we think so. For now, it seems the best we can do in an imperfect world to meet John's social needs is support him as he participates in competitive team sports. Finding another way is one of our family's greatest challenges and, we believe, one of our culture's greatest challenges.

One thing that gives us hope is the efforts of Vail Mountain School. For example, this past fall twenty-four boys signed up for the soccer team, many more than were needed. The coaches could have organized the boys into an A team (the best players) and a B team (the not-so-good players). Or, they could have asked John not to play, since he is not a student at the school. Instead, they asked all the boys to attend daily practices but to voluntarily sit out at least one of the weekly games, thus reducing the number of players for each game. Everyone was on the A team.

Similarly, during a track and field meet last spring, the children were asked to form relay teams made up of students from different schools. This eliminated competition between schools. Teams were not ranked according to first, second, third, (etc.) place and no times were kept during this meet. But, everyone had a great time.

What most gives us hope is the positive memory Denny treasures forty years later, of running fifty miles without winners or losers, and Sheila's experience in Zacatecas of everybody winning at volleyball. John's basket, Denny's run and Sheila playing volleyball all bring out what may be one of the greatest gifts of sports: to remind us that nothing is impossible, including a world of cooperation rather than competition.

# Chapter 4
# PUNISHMENT

We began the first chapter with a story about John's orange shirt strategy for addressing his fear that he would once again have a goalless soccer season. Another strategy that some parents might have tried goes something like this: "John, unless you practice harder and score more goals, we're not going to spend our time driving you to soccer anymore." Or, "John, we'll give you ten dollars for every goal you score this year." In other words, they might have used the most common methods for motivating oneself and others in our culture, which are rewards and punishments. However, John's motivation came from within himself, through what is commonly referred to as *intrinsic motivation* or *internal referencing*. Rewards and punishments, which come from outside, emphasize *extrinsic motivation* or *external referencing*.

The temptation to resort to rewards and punishments, "carrots and sticks," is very great. However, because they are external sources of motivation, they separate us from our inner compass and make us more vulnerable to societal pressures, such as the forces of consumerism and militarism that keep our system going. Yet, what alternative do we have? The majority of children in our culture are raised with rewards and punishments, most educators and employers use them, much religious teaching implies or overtly relies on them and most of us find it hard to imagine any other way of motivating human beings.

## The Chocolate

We (Denny and Sheila), too, have been tempted to resort to punishment. In our home, we eat healthy, organic food and avoid sugar. John has always known that candy is a special treat, to be eaten only at agreed-upon times. One day when John was about eight, Denny was cleaning John's closet and found a bag of chocolates hidden away there. If you were his parent, what would you do?

My (Denny's) first thought was some form of punishment, such as, "No more candy for a week...or a month...or the rest of your life!" Typically, I reverted to how my own parents would likely have handled the situation when I was a child. Fortunately, however, before I said anything to John I recalled my adult belief that punishment is rooted in efforts to control and dominate others, and is therefore dysfunctional. As Bill W., the cofounder of the Twelve-Step movement that has saved millions of people from alcoholism, said, "Punishment never heals. Only love can heal."[1] As you reflect on what you might do in a situation like this, we want to explore the roots of our culture's tendency to rely on punishment and rewards. (We'll tell you in chapter 11 how we handled the chocolate situation.)

## Why Do We Believe Punishment and Rewards Are Necessary?

Recently we gave a series of retreats in Mexico on the material in this book. We asked each of our audiences, "Do you believe people are basically good and loving, or do you believe they are selfish and violent?" In every case, the majority of people held up their hands for the selfish and violent option. Ours was not a scientific study, and we can't be sure what results we would get for the same question in the United States or other countries. However, it does seem that many people assume human beings cannot be trusted to do the right thing on their own. This leads to the belief that they must be controlled through the use of rewards and punishment. If you're "good" you'll be rewarded with a high grade, a scholarship, a raise and a big house. If you're "bad" you'll spend your life living in a slum…or a prison.

If we look around, it appears obvious that people are capable of violence and don't always behave well. Why? Is it because we're essentially selfish and destructive and haven't been punished or rewarded enough to keep us under control? If this is not the case, then why do we so often act as though it were?

## War: Here's Our Chance!…Or Is It?

War is probably the most extreme illustration of the violent side of human nature. If human beings are naturally violent and full of aggression, wouldn't they jump at the opportunity to go to war? And, once there, wouldn't they take advantage of the opportunity to kill?

In fact, people are not easily convinced to go to war. It requires a lot of propaganda, offers of financial reward and higher education for those who would otherwise probably not have the opportunity to go to college, and ultimately it may involve the last resort—the draft.

Moreover, once they are on the battlefield, soldiers behave very differently than we might think. In his book *On Killing*, Lieutenant Colonel Dave Grossman, who taught psychology at West Point, presents some remarkable research.[2] He found that, apart from a small percentage of the population who are sociopaths (estimates range from 2 to 4 percent in the western world[3]) and who may kill without remorse, the vast majority of humans will go to great lengths to avoid killing one another. From the Battle of Gettysburg through World War II, 80 or more percent of soldiers would aim their guns high, aim them low, pretend to be reloading...anything to avoid killing, even when they were being fired upon by an enemy. The other 15 to 20 percent would shoot to kill but (apart from the sociopaths) only because of the tremendous pressure they felt to do so.[4]

This is actually not new information. In 1947, a military analyst named S. L. A. Marshall, who was appointed chief historian of World War II, wrote the following after interviewing hundreds of infantry companies:

> On average not more than 15 percent of the men had actually fired at the enemy....The best showing that could be made by the most spirited and aggressive companies was that one man in four had made at least some use of his fire power....These men may face danger but they will not fight.[5]

Marshall is saying that at most one in four soldiers total—not one in four at any one time, but rather one in four *ever*—would fire their weapon even once, and he regards even that figure as generous.[6] This was true not only for new recruits but also for soldiers who had been had been through several battles.

Moreover, psychiatric studies of battle fatigue indicated that

> ...fear of killing, rather than fear of being killed, was the most common cause of battle failure in the individual....It is therefore reasonable to believe that the average and normally healthy individual—the man who can endure the physical and mental stresses of combat—still has such an inner and usually unrealized resistance toward killing a fellow man that he will not of his own volition take life if it is possible to turn away from that responsibility.[7]

This was not written by a pacifist. S. L. A. Marshall believed in the military and later became a general in the Korean War.

Military commanders who were concerned about the findings of Marshall and others initiated programs to desensitize soldiers and condition them to kill. For example, previously during target practice soldiers were given a neutrally shaped target and asked to imagine that it was an enemy combatant. Now, soldiers were given a target shaped like a human being and asked to imagine that it was a neutral object.[8] Another means of desensitization was the introduction of violent video games, which are now being used to encourage young people to join the military.[9]

These methods were very successful. The military was able to raise the killing rate from 15 or 20 percent to 65 percent by the Korean War and then to 90 or 95 percent by the Vietnam War.[10] Even so, there were 502,000 acts of desertion by U.S. military soldiers in the Vietnam War.[11]

Moreover, such programs that condition soldiers to go against their humane instincts take a toll on troops. When they return to their homes—and when they return to themselves away from the environment of desensitization and conditioning—many of these soldiers suffer from PTSD (posttraumatic stress disorder), which can result in suicide, alcoholism, drug addiction and other self-destructive behaviors.[12] In other words, we must be coerced, deceived and manipulated into violence, as in war.

Given the chance, we want what happened in 1914, on the first Christmas Eve of World War I. British, French and German troops were stationed in Belgium and France, along either side of "No Man's Land," an area about two football fields wide that marked the battle line. This basically true story has several versions. One is that Germans began to sing "Stille Nacht" ("Silent Night" in German) and British troops sang back in English. Then the Germans improvised what looked like Christmas lights. Soon a brave soldier from one side walked toward the other, holding a white flag. Instead of shooting him, someone from the other side went to meet him. Before long, their comrades had come up out of the trenches.

The two sides embraced one another, exchanged gifts, shared photos from home, played soccer and sang together. Approximately 100,000 soldiers participated in the Christmas Truce. It spread along about two-thirds or four hundred miles of the front line and lasted around two weeks, ending only when officers threatened to court-martial soldiers who "fraternized" with the enemy (a crime punishable by death in wartime).[13]

## We Are Hard-Wired for Empathy

Left to ourselves, human beings don't want to kill. Recent neurological research on *mirror neurons*, which enable us to feel what others feel, reveals that we are hard-wired for empathy. The same brain circuits that are activated when we ourselves feel pain are also activated in response to the pain of others.[14] Also, when we behave altruistically a primitive part of our brain is activated, resulting in a feeling of pleasure.[15] Moreover, it is now widely accepted that we inherited this predisposition to altruism and empathy from our primate ancestors.[16]

This innate capacity for altruism and empathy is already evident in babies. For example, if they see you drop a pen from across the room, fourteen-month-olds will climb over a pile of cushions to pick it up and give it back to you.[17] In an experiment with twenty-four eighteen-month-olds, every one of them would crawl over to help the experimenter when he dropped clothes pins or knocked over his books,

> ...but only in those instances where his facial and bodily gestures suggested...he clearly needed help, thus exhibiting a keen sensitivity to his plight and a willingness to come to his aid. The toddlers expressed a pure

> sense of altruism—offering help with no expectation of getting something in return.[18]

When our John was one year old and we were in an airport, he would sometimes hear another baby crying. He would point in the direction of the baby and say, "Mama, give John's milk."

## Why Do We Believe Humans Are Selfish and Violent?

If human beings are hard-wired for empathy, why is the world so filled with violence and war and why do we have such a negative view of human nature? Although we are predisposed to empathy, our capacity for it must be supported by the environment, beginning in earliest life. Researchers studying empathy emphasize that "parental and community nurture of infants is essential to trigger mirror neurons' circuitry and establish empathic pathways in the brain."[19] This begins in the womb and at the genetic level, since every time we receive love and empathy, our love and empathy genetic triggers are activated (see chapter 2).

Once they are born, babies need constant physical contact for many reasons, one of which is that loving touch stimulates the areas of the brain related to feelings of love and pleasure. The more those circuits are stimulated, the more they develop. When those circuits are turned on, the circuits associated with violence are turned off and their development is inhibited.[20] James Prescott studied forty-nine societies in terms of how much loving touch children experienced and how much violence existed among adults. He found that societies with more loving touch had less violence and societies with less loving touch had more violence.[21]

Beyond the family, comes the social environment or field (more about this in chapters 7 and 10) in which we live as adults. Neuroscientist Marco Iacoboni suggests that

> ...externally manipulated, massive belief systems, including political ideologies, tend to override the unconscious, pre-reflective, neurobiological traits that should bring us together. For example, the fear-mongering of artificially created global scarcity may attenuate our empathic response. Another is the military's refusal to allow putting a face on the U.S. wounded and dead soldiers in Iraq. As Professor Robert Jensen puts it, "The way we are educated and entertained keeps us from knowing about or understanding the pain of others."[22]

## Survival of the Fittest?

One of the belief systems in which most of us have been educated that contributes to our view of human nature is a misunderstanding of Darwin. When we think of Darwin, the first words that commonly come to mind (besides *evolution*) are *survival of the fittest.* We usually take this to mean that living creatures are engaged in a heartless struggle with one another for survival, in which the strong make it only by conquering the weak.

As it turns out, Darwin, too, believed that we are hard-wired for empathy. In his book, *The Descent of Man*, Darwin focuses not on prehuman evolution but rather on what drives our own species at our level of development. Dr. David Loye did a word search of the 475 pages of *The Descent of Man*, and he found the phrase *survival of the fittest* exactly once, where Darwin was apologizing for using the term. In that same book, Darwin writes about love ninety-five times (even though Loye found only one entry for *love* in the index), and he writes about moral sensitivity ninety-two times (Loye found only six entries in the index). Darwin believed the prime mover of human evolution is not natural selection nor survival of the fittest, but rather our capacity for love, caring for one another and moral sensitivity (our sense of right vs. wrong).[23]

Why does this matter so much? It matters because Darwin's theory—and our misunderstanding of it—is one of the primary influences on modern civilization and on our understanding of what it means to be a human being. Human beings are social; we learn who we are according to who our family and society tell us we are, and we treat ourselves and others accordingly. If we think we are basically selfish and violent, we don't trust ourselves or anyone else. People then tend to fulfill our negative expectations of them. Moreover, our negative projections may blind us to the good intentions of others. Either way, we end up believing we need to punish or reward people to control them. In a sort of self-fulfilling misunderstanding of Darwin, we can then justify all kinds of economic and political systems of domination of our weaker members by our stronger ones.

## Blue Eyes/Brown Eyes

One of the most graphic illustrations of how vulnerable we are to this cycle of being told who we are and then acting accordingly is a classic social science experiment known as "Blue Eyes/Brown Eyes." This originated with Jane Elliott, a third-grade teacher in a small town in Iowa in the 1960s, where everyone was white and Christian.[24]

After the assassination of Martin Luther King, Jane wanted a way to help her third-graders understand prejudice. So, she devised an experiment. She began class one day by telling her students,

> Today, the blue-eyed people will be on the bottom and the brown-eyed people on the top. What I mean is that brown-eyed people are better than blue-eyed people. They are cleaner than blue-eyed people. They

> are more civilized than blue-eyed people. And they are smarter than blue-eyed people.[25]

She told the brown-eyed children that only they could have five extra minutes at recess, use the big playground equipment, go first to lunch and return for second helpings. And, Jane said, "Blue-eyed people are not allowed to play with brown-eyed people unless they are invited." She instructed the blue-eyed children to sit in the back of the room, and gave each brown-eyed child a collar to put on a blue-eyed child.

Throughout the day, every time a brown-eyed child got the right answer in class or did almost anything, Jane would say, "See! Brown-eyed children are smart and they do things right." Every time a blue-eyed child made a mistake, she would say, "What do you expect?! That's just how blue-eyed children are!" By lunchtime, it was obvious whether a child was blue- or brown-eyed:

> The brown-eyed children were happy, alert, having the time of their lives. And they were doing far better work than they had ever done before. The blue-eyed children were miserable. Their posture, their expressions, their entire attitudes were those of defeat. Their classroom work regressed sharply from that of the day before. Inside of an hour or so, they looked and acted as if they were, in fact, inferior. It was shocking.
>
> But even more frightening was the way the brown-eyed children turned on their friends of the day before....[26]

The next day, Jane reversed the experiment and this time she labeled the blue-eyed ones as superior. The same thing happened in reverse. At the end of the day, she told the children it was only an experiment and there was no innate difference between blue-eyed and brown-eyed people. The children took off their collars and hugged one another, looking immensely relieved to be equals and friends again.

An interesting aspect of the experiment is how it affected learning. Jane tested the children on spelling, math and reading two weeks before the experiment, on both days of it and two weeks after it was over. Their scores went up on the day they were superior, down on the day they were inferior, and then stayed higher than before the experiment for the rest of the year. Jane did not understand this, and so she sent the test scores to Stanford University for evaluation. Stanford responded that it seemed as if the children's academic ability had changed in one day, but they could not explain how this was possible. Here's how Jane explained it to herself:

> On the day they are in the "superior" group and doing genuinely superior work, they find out for the first time what their true potential is. They learn by actual experience that they can do much better work than they have been doing.... They don't just *think* they can do better work; they *know* they can because they have.[27]

In other words, once the children realized that their power to learn depended on their belief in themselves, they held on to believing they were smart and didn't let go of it again.

The point of this experiment is that our sense of who we are comes in large part from believing what the environment tells us about ourselves. Recall the words of Einstein: "The field is the sole governing principle of the particle." If we live in a field of negativity, if the environment holds up an ugly picture and tells us it's a mirror, we're likely to believe the ugly picture and behave like it. Our culture gives us reason for self-hatred, by constantly holding up ugly pictures and telling us they are mirrors. It's very like Jane Elliott putting collars on all of us to continually remind us that we're selfish and destructive.

We are all "culturally hypnotized from birth"[28] to believe this. Much of it comes through the media and the entertainment industry, where we see ever-increasing levels of violence, despite all the evidence that has been collected for decades that watching this stuff makes children unfeeling, aggressive and fearful. Dr. Marco Iacoboni says that actually we are so "wired for empathy" that "If we could stop all the violence for a week, it would never come back."[29] He believes that just one week away from all the artificial provocation to violence would make such a difference in our culture that the rest of the problem could eventually be brought down to very minimal levels. If enough of us did this, we'd be on our way to living in a nonviolent culture. We would no longer see ourselves as selfish and destructive, nor as needing to be controlled through the use of rewards and punishment. Like Jane Elliott's third-graders, when the experiment was over and the brown collars were taken off, we'd remember that we were made for love and connection.

In his book *Ancestral Grace*, Diarmuid O'Murchu puts this into a much larger, seven-million-year context that includes our human and protohuman ancestors. Archaeological research suggests that for most of this long history, humans lived in cooperative relationships with one another and with their earth environment. This changed only about ten thousand years ago as we distanced ourselves from the earth, coupled with the emergence of a patriarchal domination system that increasingly pervaded much of human civilization. Ten thousand years is a tiny percentage of our time as an intelligent, creative species. Yet, we identify with and define ourselves by this more violent period of our history. Even in the field of primate research, we see ourselves more as relatives of the relatively competitive and aggressive chimpanzees rather than the peaceful bonobos, to whom we may actually be closer temperamentally. Researchers who study human nature only in terms of the past several thousand years miss the rest of our long history. They also often miss the effects upon us of more recent systemic and social forces identified by people like Marco Iacoboni and Jane Elliott, such as the media and entertainment industry and the effects of racial prejudice. These forces deceive us into believing we are innately selfish and destructive. As O'Murchu puts it, when we think in terms of seven million rather than ten thousand years, "the evidence of the larger story suggests that *we got it right for most of our time as an earth-based species*."[30]

However, most of us live in a culture where the emphasis is on all the ways we've gotten it wrong and where rewards and punishment pervade everyday life. To get in touch with how this may separate us from our light, we suggest the following imagination exercise.

## PUNISHMENT NEVER HEALS

1. Close your eyes. Imagine yourself as a five-year-old child.
2. Pull a chair over to a high cupboard or shelf where your mother keeps a hidden box of chocolates. You know she does not want you to have them. Reach up on your tiptoes for the chocolates. As you grab the box, you accidentally hit one of your mother's favorite cups and it goes crashing to the ground.
3. What do you do? Do you eat the candy? Do you go and tell your mother what happened?

When we lead retreatants in this exercise, almost nobody eats the candy and even fewer people tell their mother. I (Denny) imagine myself sweeping up all the evidence of the broken cup, throwing it in the wastebasket and putting a large milk carton on top to hide the broken pieces. Then I go outside to play as if nothing had happened. A short time later, my mother calls me to come into the kitchen. As I enter, she is looking down at the floor. She says, "What's this?" I say, "What's what?" because there is nothing there. I don't understand how mothers can see what no longer exists. Then my mother pulls me over to the wastebasket. I say, "Oh, that. I was going to prepare you a cup of tea and when I opened up the cupboard, the cup came crashing to the ground."

Notice that I did not tell the truth. The healthy thing would have been for me to admit my guilt and say, "I was trying to take a piece of candy and I accidentally hit your cup. I'm sorry." Then we could have talked about it. If my mother had been able to draw out the story behind my behavior, we might have found an appropriate way to meet my needs. Once we understood each other, our gratitude for one another would have been restored. Then, it would have been easy for my mother to forgive me and I would have been able to forgive myself, especially if we could have agreed on a suitable way for me to make amends.

But, instead of acting in a healthy way, I buried my guilt and I lied. I did that because I feared my mother's punishment. She was known as "the Little General," and she punished us by spanking us with a stick. I spent a lot of my childhood hiding her sticks.

Punishment evokes fear, which destroys trust. When we are punished, we no longer feel safe to use our voice and express what is deepest within us. In my case, I buried my guilt, the story of my behavior was not heard and my needs were not met. Buried guilt can lead to depression and scrupulosity, in which we wrongly assume that everything is our fault. I suffered from both. Not only does punishment compromise our emotional health; it also leads to broken relationships, at the very time when we most need to feel connected to others so that the needs underlying our behavior can be met. As social psychologist Alfie Kohn says, we are about as grateful to see the person who administers punishment as we are to see a police officer in our rearview mirror.[31]

Although we may have been taught that the fear of punishment is necessary to motivate people to be "good," this works only in the short run. It works because fear is likely to make us more compliant. If I am a child and you are twice as big as me, and you threaten to hit me or punish me in some other way, I will do what you say. But I have not learned to understand or appreciate the story underlying my behavior, or the needs I was trying to meet, or how to grow in truly loving behavior. I have learned only how to placate you and avoid being punished. I have stopped listening to my own inner voice, and the only voice I can hear is yours.

## Punishment Undermines Inner Strength

Let's suppose that I (Denny) had not restrained my temptation to punish John for the hidden chocolate I found in his closet. And let's suppose our normal method of parenting involved punishment for any behavior we viewed as "disobedient." John, who is very loving and values human connection above all else, would likely develop the same pattern I had, of trying to placate others—especially those who speak with a strong voice. Suppose further that an adult who conveys authority (a coach, a priest, etc.) then tried to sexually abuse him. Where would John find the inner strength to resist? And when he was sixteen and someone offered him illegal drugs, how would he find the voice to say, "No!"? And when he was eighteen and a military recruiter tried to recruit him for an unjust war, how would John maintain contact with the values of peace, love and justice that are so congruent with his nature?

As many people have observed, it is no accident that religious groups such as Focus on the Family, which emphasize obedience to authority and teach punishment (including corporal punishment) as an acceptable form of parenting, are the same groups that adamantly supported the Iraq War (see chapter 6). As moral theologian Bernard Haring wrote,

> What most influenced my thinking about moral theology was the mindless and criminal obedience of Christians to Hitler, a madman and tyrant. This led me to the conviction that the character of a Christian must not be formed one-sidedly by a leitmotif of obedience but rather by a discerning responsibility, a capacity to respond courageously to new values and new needs, and a readiness to take the risk.[32]

Although punishment might encourage obedience, in the long run it does not encourage genuine goodness any more than it encouraged Denny to tell the truth. When we are frightened we are less likely to trust our most generous instincts. For example, in their research on altruism, Samuel and Pearl Oliner studied Polish Christians who risked their lives to rescue Jews during World War II. One characteristic these rescuers shared was that their parents rarely if ever punished them in childhood. Their parents emphasized high standards of moral and ethical behavior, but used reason and their own example rather than punishment to guide their children.[33]

The result was that these people had a high level of what the Oliners called *extensivity*, meaning the capacity to include people different from themselves (such as Jews) in their circle of care. They were able to resist pressure from peers and authorities that ran counter to their values of compassion for all, and they refused to participate in "the silence of good people."

## Healing Process: Experiences of Punishment

1. Sit comfortably, close your eyes and place your hand on your heart. Let your awareness go down into your heart and imagine that you are breathing in and out through your heart.
2. Recall a time when you were punished.
3. What do you notice in your body as you recall this experience? What emotions do you feel? Take a moment to lovingly care for yourself, perhaps moving your hand to the part of your body that most needs attention. Breathe in whatever you most need.
4. How did this experience affect your relationship with the person who punished you? How did this experience affect your life at the time? Does it still affect you in any way today?
5. How would you handle the same situation if you were the parent or other caregiver? Imagine caring for yourself in this way, as you continue to breathe deeply.

Chapter 5

# REWARDS

Many of us grew up being scolded, penalized or spanked when we were "bad." When we were "good," we received As, gold stars, toys and candy. Although rewards may seem like a nicer way to motivate people than punishment, they are no more effective in the long run. One of the most thoroughly researched areas of social psychology is the extent to which rewards extinguish intrinsic motivation. If you offer me a reward, I may well do what you want. But, as with punishment, I have not learned to understand or appreciate myself, nor you, nor the real reasons to do what is good. I have learned only how to please you and get the reward.

In his book *Punished by Rewards*, Alfie Kohn has collected some of the numerous studies demonstrating the ineffectiveness of rewards.[1] These studies show that the more we reward another person for doing something, the less interest that person will have in continuing the behavior when we cease giving the reward. For example, if two groups of people want to stop smoking and we offer the members of the first group twenty dollars for each day they don't smoke, they will smoke less than the second group who receives nothing. However, as soon as we stop giving the first group twenty dollars a day, they will smoke *more* than the second group.[2]

Note that rewards are quite different from celebration. For example, early in our home-school reading program, when John got halfway through the alphabet, we celebrated by taking him out for pizza. But we never used pizza as a way to motivate him; we never told him, "*If* you learn the alphabet, *then* we'll take you out for pizza." Rather, by the time we got to M, we were all having so much fun that we wanted to celebrate. (A well-known pizza chain has a program known as "Book It!" in which they offer free pizzas to children who read a certain number of books each month. As one astute educator commented, the likely result is "…a lot of fat kids who don't like to read,"[3] not to mention the chain's profit from all the extra pizzas bought by parents and grandparents who accompany the child to the restaurant.) The difference between celebration and rewards is intention. The intention of celebration is to express gratitude. The intention of rewards is to control the other person.

A subtle form of reward that we might mistake for gratitude is praise. For example, if John and a group of his friends are playing in our home and I (Sheila) say to the children, "I really like the way Chris is cleaning up," my intention is probably to manipulate all the children into imitating Chris, rather than to convey genuine gratitude. Similarly, if I (Denny) say to Sheila, "That's a great dinner," I convey a judgment of Sheila's cooking, albeit a positive one. However, if I say to her, "Thanks for the dinner you made. I was really hungry and tired when I came home. Now I feel alive again," I have conveyed gratitude in an authentic and vulnerable way.

Genuine expressions of gratitude include acknowledging the behavior of the person for whom we are grateful, the need that was met in ourselves and the pleasurable feelings we have as a result of our need being met: "This is what you did…this is the need you met in me…this is how I feel." Our intention is to reveal ourselves rather than to control or manipulate the other.[4]

Manipulative and/or judgmental praise and rewards in general are forms of extrinsic motivation, which is based upon "should." Rewards diminish intrinsic motivation, which is based upon gratitude for ourselves and for others. Intrinsic motivation is much more powerful and enduring than extrinsic motivation.

There are several reasons why rewards diminish intrinsic motivation. One is that, surprising as it may seem, rewards are a form of domination and control. They are just as coercive as punishment. Rewards might be called "control through seduction," and few of us like to be controlled.[5]

Another reason rewards diminish intrinsic motivation is that they devalue the behavior we are trying to encourage. For example, if I (Sheila) say to John, "Do your math problems, honey, and I'll take you out to a movie," John thinks, "If she has to bribe me to do math, it must not be worth doing." I have not helped John to appreciate the wonders of math.[6]

## Rewards Keep Us from Living in the Present

Rewards also focus our attention on getting something in the future and distract us from living from within ourselves in the present. I (Matt) have seen this very clearly in myself, especially in my attitude toward work. I am the oldest child and was taught that I should be responsible. I worked hard in school because I believed I should get As rather than Bs, so that I could get into a good college so that I could get a well-paying job so that I could take care of a family and eventually retire comfortably. After school, I worked hard on my paper route because I believed I should save up money "for a rainy day."

As often happens, all my careful planning for the future was useless. I didn't get married and raise a family. Instead, I joined the Jesuits…where I began the same cycle all over again. Even now, I always wear a watch so that I can get the most work done in the least amount of time. I save my airplane peanuts because I should have some on hand in case there's a drought and the world's food supply fails. Because I believe I should prepare for the future, I often miss gratefully enjoying the present moment.

Denny, being younger, observed what was happening to me and, by the end of high school, decided to opt out of rewards. All through his theology studies, he never opened his report cards because he wanted to be free to learn what was important to him rather than what was rewarded by good grades. He doesn't wear a watch because he gratefully enjoys the present moment rather than worrying about what he should do in the future. He eats his peanuts on the plane and usually asks for more. In other words, I work hard and Denny hardly works. When I am doing something because I should rather than because I enjoy it, it probably means I have been hooked by the desire for rewards (or the fear of punishment).

Alfie Kohn recounts a story that captures very well how manipulative rewards can be and how far they can take us from intrinsic motivation:

> It is the story of an elderly man who endured the insults of a crowd of ten-year-olds each day as they passed his house on their way home from school. One afternoon, after listening to another round of jeers about how stupid and ugly and bald he was, the man came up with a plan. He met the children on his lawn the following Monday and announced that anyone who came back the next day and yelled rude comments about him would receive a dollar. Amazed and excited, they showed up even earlier on Tuesday, hollering epithets for all they were worth. True to his word, the old man ambled out and paid everyone. "Do the same tomorrow," he told them, "and you'll get twenty-five cents for your trouble." The kids thought that was still pretty good and turned out again on Wednesday to

taunt him. At the first catcall, he walked over with a roll of quarters and again paid off his hecklers. "From now on," he announced, "I can give you only a penny for doing this." The kids looked at each other in disbelief. "A penny?" they repeated scornfully. "Forget it!" And they never came back again.[7]

## Healing Process: Do Rewards Really Motivate You?

1. Close your eyes and breathe deeply. Put your hand on your heart and imagine that you are breathing through your heart.
2. Recall a time when you did something because you wanted a reward (money, a toy or other material object, good grades, a promotion, praise, etc.) rather than because you truly wanted to do it. Notice how you feel when you recall that experience. Hold these feelings in your heart and let them speak to you as you continue to breathe deeply.
3. Recall a time when you did something solely because you wanted to. Notice how you feel when you recall that experience. Hold these feelings in your heart and let them speak to you as you continue to breathe deeply.
4. What do these two experiences tell you about something you are doing now that you are not enjoying? What do they tell you about how you want to live your life in the future?

## Chapter 6

# SOMEONE HAS TO PAY

One of the reasons for the prevalence of rewards and punishment in our culture is religious teaching. This is how Denny and Matt's mother became "the Little General" and why they spent so much of their childhood hiding her sticks. Agnes May Linn was raised in a deeply religious Roman Catholic culture that took literally Proverbs 13:24, "spare the rod and spoil the child." Parents who cared for their children truly believed they should spank them as an expression of love.

However, as psychoanalyst Alice Miller writes,

> "He who spares the rod hates his son, but he who loves him is diligent to discipline him," we read in Proverbs. This so-called wisdom is still so widespread today that we can often hear: "A slap given in love does a child no harm."...If people weren't accustomed to the biblical injunction from childhood, it would strike them as the untruth it is. Cruelty is the opposite of love, and its traumatic effect, far from being reduced, is actually reinforced if it is presented as a sign of love....No one ever slaps a child out of love but rather because in similar situations, when one was defenseless, one was slapped and then compelled to interpret it as a sign of love....
>
> If a mother can make it clear to a child that at that particular moment when she slapped him, her love for him deserted her and she was dominated by other

> feelings that had nothing to do with the child, the child can keep a clear head, feel respected, and not be disoriented in his relationship to his mother.[1]

Spanking is only one of the many ways that religious teaching has contributed to the pervasive use of rewards and punishments throughout our culture. The Bible is interpreted to justify many forms of violent punishment of those who displease us, whether it be hitting your own child or killing hundreds of thousands of children (and their parents) in other countries upon whom we declare war. According to biblical scholar Raymond Schwager, the Hebrew Bible contains

> ...one thousand verses where God's own violent actions of punishment are described, a hundred passages where Yahweh expressly commands others to kill people, and several stories where God kills or tries to kill for no apparent reason....Violence...is easily the most often mentioned activity and central theme of the Hebrew Bible.[2]

Meanwhile, the obedient Israelites who carry out God's punitive commands will be rewarded with abundant life in the Promised Land. When we project our notions of personhood onto the ultimate mystery of the universe, as happens when we read the Bible literally, God is a "somebody" and that somebody is on *our* side. George W. Bush, who frequently affirmed his reliance on the Christian Bible for guidance during his presidency, was quoted as saying "God told me to strike at al Qaida and I struck them, and then he instructed me to strike at Saddam, which I did."[3]

The New Testament fares no better in the hands of those who believe in punishment and rewards. Thoughtful and otherwise loving people will shake their heads sadly and assure us that it's all too bad, but the end times are near and anyone who doesn't "accept Jesus" will be punished with destruction, while the "believers" will be swept up into heaven in "the rapture." In a 2004 poll, 55 percent of respondents agreed with this.[4]

In contrast, Gandhi, who read the Sermon on the Mount every morning, once said, "Jesus was the most active nonviolent resister known to history. But the only people who don't know that Jesus was nonviolent are Christians."[5] Echoing Gandhi and in response to Bush's declaration of war against Afghanistan (a war the United States Catholic Bishops' Conference supported), Jesuit priest Daniel Berrigan said,

> We should just burn our copies of the Gospels, process into our church sanctuaries holding aloft the *Air Force Rule Book*, with its command to kill our enemies, and incense that instead. At least that would be more honest. It would express our fidelity to the god of war, since we do not worship the god of peace.[6]

## Torture??

A consequence of this that shocked us was a recent survey of Americans' attitudes toward torture. The survey found that, "The more often Americans go to church, the more likely they are to support the torture of suspected terrorists...."[7] Christians supporting torture??

In an effort to understand this, the former president of Chicago Theological Seminary, Susan Brooks Thistlethwaite, suggested a theological explanation: the belief that Jesus paid for our sins by undergoing the torture of being flogged and crucified.[8] This belief was glorified in Mel Gibson's movie, *The Passion of the Christ*. The message is that severe pain and suffering are central to Christian faith, we really are selfish and violent, and somebody has to be punished to pay for that. For many Christians this message gets reinforced every Sunday. Is it true?

It may be helpful to understand the thinking behind this message, which comes in part from the influence of a medieval theologian named Anselm (1033–1109). For the sake of dramatic effect, theologian Walter Imbiorski caricatures Anselm's literal interpretation of certain passages of the Bible as follows:

> You see, part of the difficulty is that most of us are caught up emotionally in what I would call Anselmian salvation theology, which goes something like this. God created the world. Adam and Eve sinned. God got pretty damn sore, goes into a 10,000-year pout, slams the gates of heaven and throws the scoundrels out. So he's up there pouting and about 5,000 years go by and the Son comes up and gives him the elbow and says: "Hey Dad, now is the time to forgive those people down there." God says, "No. I don't like them, they offended my divine majesty, they stay out. Let's make another galaxy instead!" Five thousand more years go by and the Son comes up and says: "Aw come on, Dad, let's forgive them! Look, I tell you what I'm going to do. If you will love them again, I'll go down there and become one of them, then you'll have to love them because I'll be one of them." God looks at the Son and says: "Don't bank on it. That doesn't turn me on too much at all." So the Son replies, "All right, God-Father, I'll tell you what I'm going to do. I'll raise the ante. I'll make you an offer you can't refuse! I'll not only go down there and become one of them, I'll suffer for them, real blood—you know how that turns you on, Dad! How about it?" And God says: "Now you're talking. But it's got to be real torture and real blood—no God-tricks you understand. You've

> got to really suffer. And if you'll do that then I'll forgive them. But if they stray off the straight and narrow just that much—ZAP—I'm going to send them to hell so fast their heads will swim." And that is what we have been calling the "good news" of the Gospel.[9]

Although here carried to its extreme, this is a form of thinking that many of us grew up with, known as *Anselmian salvation (or satisfaction) theology*. Most Christians would probably be shocked, as we were, to learn that this is not and never has been the doctrine of the Church nor did Jesus ever teach it. Referring to Anselmian salvation theology, theologian Richard McBrien writes, "It was never made an official teaching of the Church....Over the years, many Catholics have incorrectly assumed it to be a matter of doctrine, if not even of dogma."[10]

Perhaps the experience of mothers can help us. If you are a mother, recall the pain you felt during the birth of one of your children. Did you say to your baby, "You caused me so much pain that I am not going to love you until you make it up to me?"

Anselm unfortunately was not a mother. He lived in the eleventh century, when honor was very important. If you offended the king, you had to make satisfaction to him through public amends. Otherwise, you were put in the dungeon or even killed. Anselm believed Adam and Eve had offended the infinite King, God, and so someone had to make infinite amends. However, as limited human beings we could not make infinite amends and we, therefore, were in God's dungeon with the gates of heaven closed. To Anselm's way of thinking, Jesus was the only one who could make satisfaction to this God through an infinite sacrifice of his life on the cross.

However, Anselmian satisfaction theology represents only one of the possible understandings of Jesus' death.[11] For example, New Testament professor Donald Senior summarizes the gospel writers as follows:

> ...the ultimate reason for Jesus' death was the way he lived. His commitment to the poor and the marginalized, the priority he gave to alleviating human pain, his confrontation with injustice—these are the things that stoked opposition to Jesus and ultimately led to his death.[12]

The twelfth-century theologian Peter Abelard took a different point of view than had Anselm, described as follows by Joseph Campbell: "Jesus' death on the cross was not as ransom paid, or as a penalty applied, but an act of atonement, at-one-ment, with the race."[13] By becoming "at one" with the suffering of life, Jesus evokes the human sentiment of compassion. His cross invites us to focus our hearts on compassionately living for one another. When we live in this way, we want everyone's needs to be met rather than trying to control one another through the use of rewards and punishment.

## We All Get What We Need

To illustrate Jesus' attitude, at retreats we like to act out his story of the workers in the vineyard (Matt 20:1–16). Sheila plays the owner of the vineyard (a modern owner who drives a truck with a loud horn that honks as she goes back and forth picking up workers at various hours of the day). Volunteers from the audience play the workers, some of whom work all day and others only an hour. John plays the foreman who pays everyone the same amount at the end of the day and gets yelled at by those who came early and believe they should get more.

When the story is finished, we ask our audience, "Is it fair that those who worked only one hour in the cool of the evening receive the same wages as those who worked perhaps twelve hours, and through the heat of the day?" Most audiences are divided about evenly, some saying it is fair and others saying it isn't.

Their confusion is understandable, because we really can't answer such a question without knowing the historical context. This story takes place on the final day of the harvest season, and it involves a race against time to gather the grapes before freezing weather comes at nightfall and ruins them. Thus, the strongest and best workers are hired first. Those hired last are the drunks, the lazy, the ex-convicts, in other words, the worst workers and/or those who are not trusted. They are so grateful to be hired at all that, unlike those hired first, that they do not even ask for a contract.

Daniel Harrington, regarded by many as the world's expert on Matthew's gospel, says that the images used here—final harvest, vineyard, settling of accounts—identify this passage as a parable about the final judgment.[14] Each worker receives one denarius, which was the amount of money needed to survive for one day. Thus, the parable is saying that in the end everyone receives what he or she needs.

Perhaps this emphasis on receiving what we need is why, during the first three centuries of Christianity, the most quoted scripture passage was: "God makes the sun shine over the good and the bad and sends the rain over the just and the unjust" (Matt 5:45).[15] In other words, we live in a universe, not of rewards and punishments, but of generosity and abundance.[a]

---

[a]If we are neither punished nor rewarded, does this mean our actions have no consequences? Do cruel dictators, mass murderers, drug dealers and abusers of the young get to enjoy the next life equally with the saints of this world who have given their lives in loving service of others? As in the case of the parable of the workers, at first glance it doesn't seem fair.

Perhaps psychiatrist Dr. Raymond Moody can help us. Moody is regarded as the "father of near-death studies" and is best known for his classic book on the subject, *Life after Life* (Covington GA: Mockingbird, 1975). He has interviewed thousands of people who have had near-death experiences. During a presentation with Dr. Melvin Morse entitled "Near Death Experiences" (Boulder CO: Sounds True Recordings, 1991), in response to a question as to whether he had ever heard of a negative or "hellish" near-death experience, Moody said "No." He added that he had encountered two cases of very negative experiences, but in each case the person was delirious. Delirium is a state of loss of contact with reality, whereas a near-death experience is more real than ordinary reality.

The last time we presented the story of the vineyard was during a retreat in Mexico. At the end of the day, John was hungry. Across the street from where we were staying was a small taco stand, run by a family. We'd been watching the stand each evening and wondered how the family could survive with so few customers. So, John was excited that he could give the owner some business, and he offered to treat us all to tacos. He went across the street to the stand and stayed for a long time. As we watched him from the window, we saw him talking to the parents and playing with their children.

When John finally did return, he was even more excited about the big tip he gave the father of the family than about the tacos. He explained that the father needed to buy more fuel for his stove, and John's tip would give the family what they needed for their business to survive another day. Like the owner of the vineyard, John understood that everyone should get what he or she needs.

## Process for Healing Scripture

1. Close your eyes and sit comfortably with your feet flat on the floor. Put your hand on your heart and breathe deeply. Imagine that you are breathing in and out through your heart.

---

In the same presentation, Moody described an aspect of the near-death experience known as the *life review*, which may take place in the presence of a Being of Light. Most of us think of the life review as seeing our life flash before us, as if on a movie screen. Actually, according to Moody, we see our entire life at once as "a kind of panorama," in full color, three dimensions and as if from a third-person point of view. Moreover, we experience the effect we had upon those we interacted with during our life; we feel the joy of those to whom we were kind and loving, as well as the suffering of those to whom we were unkind and unloving.

Those who return from such experiences are usually greatly changed for the good. Moody gives examples of people who might previously have been diagnosed as sociopaths and who returned with genuine love and compassion for others. Significantly, those who experience the life review report that they did not feel they were being punished. Rather, they experienced it as an opportunity to learn responsibility and grow in love and compassion. In other words, they received what they needed.

2. If you were raised in a religious tradition, recall a passage of scripture or a teaching by a religious authority that justified violence.
3. What effect did this have upon you? How did you feel and what did you need? Where do you still carry that in your body? Put your hand on that place and give it a loving, caring presence. Breathe in what you need.
4. If you were writing that scripture or giving that teaching, what would you say?

Chapter 7

# THE TRANCE

When we play musical chairs with retreat groups and begin by asking our volunteers to play the usual, competitive way, everyone complies. No one seems to wonder why there need to be six losers and only one winner. Why do we so easily accept ways of doing things that separate us from our light?

Perhaps a starting point is something we noticed a while ago when we signed onto our internet service provider, AOL.com. As usual, the opening page flashed about eight headlines in rapid succession. One of the first that day was something like, "Bomb Kills 20 in Baghdad." Next came, "New Handbags for Spring." This happens all the time. A newscaster announces how many were killed in a bloody battle in the same tone of voice as the scores for a football game. It was quite notable when Walter Cronkite's voice broke on national television in 1963 as he announced the death of John F. Kennedy, because newscasters never show emotion.

The dissonance of bombs and handbags in the same news report creates a sense of unreality and even dissociation that desensitizes us to violence. In order to take this in, we have to be in a trance. Or, perhaps taking this in puts us into a trance because it is so surreal. People in a trance easily lose touch with their essence and with their innate love and wisdom.

## How Are Human Beings Entranced?

Several years ago, we were involved in an educational program with a group of friends that was taught by a person we will call "Pat," a professional in a field related to ours who had dazzling skills. Eventually we discovered that Pat was habitually lying and had lost a professional license due to charges of unethical behavior—behavior Pat later repeated. As coordinators of the program, it was our responsibility to tell group members that our teacher had been lying to us. We thought they would be shocked and perhaps even blame us. But, one by one, group members said, "I never trusted Pat," or "You're finally naming something I sensed all along."

Why had no one spoken up before? Why did we ourselves not speak up during a group meeting in which we knew perfectly well that Pat was lying to us all?

Looking back, we realize that we were in a trance. Pat was charming and promised all sorts of things, most of all to be the mother or father that many of us had never had. Pat gave the impression of being the perfect parent who understood our deepest needs as no one else could and who would help us fill those needs. Each of us was vulnerable to Pat in a different way, depending on the stage of development at which our needs were not met.

We began coming out of the trance when we listened to an inner voice we had ignored that had been telling us all along, "Something is wrong." Sharing this with others who validated us helped us become willing to face the truth about Pat. Next, we found ways to meet the needs that had made us so vulnerable. Only then was the trance really broken and only then were we able to confront the situation and encourage Pat to get professional help.

A related example is the televised testimony of a Kuwaiti girl who was introduced to the American public as "Nurse Nayirah." She testified before a congressional committee prior to the first Gulf War, in October, 1990. Tearfully she said, "While I was there [in Kuwait] I saw the Iraqi soldiers come into the hospital with guns. They took the babies out of incubators, took the incubators, and left the children to die on the cold floor."[1] President George H. W. Bush expressed outrage on national television, with the implication that military action against Iraq would be a defense of helpless babies. The United States was the good mother who would protect babies from the cruel Iraqis.

Since most adult Americans were raised by parents who believed in leaving babies to cry in their cribs for fear of spoiling them, most of us would likely identify with the plight of neglected babies. Anger at what happened to us could be directed at the Iraqis, and unconsciously we might hope that the baby in each of us whose basic needs had not been met would finally be protected as well.

The problem with all this is that the Kuwaiti girl was lying. Kuwaiti babies were not pulled from their incubators and she was not a nurse. She was actually the daughter of the Kuwaiti ambassador. The American public relations firm of Hill and Knowlton told her what to say and coached her in acting (including when to shed tears). However, the story was repeated over and over by the first President Bush, as part of a campaign designed to entrance the American public into supporting the first Gulf War. It worked. Support by the U.S. public for military action soared, and three months later, in January, 1991, Operation Desert Storm began.[2]

## Car Dealers and Governments Know How to Entrance Us

Advertising firms know that the best way to put us into a trance is by appealing to our primal needs, as Pat and George H. W. Bush did. Whether used by car dealers or governments, the techniques are the same:[3]

1. Generate disorientation. We hear "bombs" and "new handbags" in quick succession, and we feel disoriented because we don't know how to hold the horror of the one and the frivolity of the other in the same moment of awareness. Pat generated disorientation by encouraging us to begin training sessions by getting

in touch with our most traumatic memories. George H. W. Bush conjured up the shocking image of newborn babies dying on a cold, hard floor.

2. Induce regression. This means putting people in touch with very young aspects of themselves by appealing to primitive feelings and needs, such as fear and the need for safety. For example, Pat encouraged us to relive our traumatic memories with all the attendant emotions, and Nurse Nayirah's story reminded us of what it was like to be left to cry alone as babies.
3. Become the target's transferred parent figure who promises to provide protection and care, as Pat did with our group and as George H. W. Bush did with our nation.

We can understand why a car dealer would want to put us into a trance: to sell us a car. Why would the media, from the headlines on the internet to national television news programs, participate in this? To what end are we bombarded with messages that put us into a trance, thereby separating us from our light, from our love and wisdom? Who benefits from this collective trance in which we are encouraged to believe that the toxicity of our culture with all its violence and materialism is just the way human beings are?

Robert F. Kennedy Jr.'s research suggests an answer. Speaking in 2004, he said:

> ...there are five giant multi-national corporations who control virtually all 14,000 radio stations in America, all 5,000 television stations, 80 percent of our newspapers, all of our billboards and most of the large internet content. So there are five guys who are deciding what we hear as news and information.[4]

The members of the boards of directors of the corporations that own our media are also on the boards of weapons manufacturers.[5] For example, NBC is owned by General Electric, which is the country's third largest military contractor. GE produces parts for every nuclear weapon in the U.S. arsenal, makes jet engines for military aircraft and creates all kinds of profitable electronic gadgets for the Pentagon. This means GE and NBC have a vested interest in militarism:

> Top executives at GE have long been aware that in order to keep billions of Pentagon dollars flowing into its coffers it was necessary to build public support for massive military spending. In 1950, President Truman named Charles Wilson, GE's board chairman, to head the Office of Defense Mobilization. In that capacity, Wilson told members of the Newspaper Publishers Association: "If the people were not convinced [that the Free World is in mortal danger] it would be impossible for Congress to vote the vast sums now being spent to avert this danger. With the support of public opinion, as marshaled by the press, we are off to a good start. It is our job—yours and mine—to keep our people convinced that the only way to keep disaster away from our shores is to build up America's might."[6]

Such information clearly suggests that it is what President Eisenhower called the "military-industrial complex" that benefits from our entrancement. It also confirms what former CIA director William Colby stated so bluntly: "The Central Intelligence Agency owns everyone of any significance in the major media."[7]

Methods of government manipulation of the media are based upon the techniques of modern propaganda first developed by Edward Bernays, the American nephew of Sigmund Freud. In his book *Propaganda*, published in 1928, Bernays wrote that the "intelligent manipulation of the organized habits and opinions of the masses was an important element in democratic society" and that the manipulators "constitute an invisible government which is the true ruling power in our country." Instead of propaganda, he coined the euphemism *public relations.* Bernays believed that "engineering public consent" was for the greater good. This was achieved by the creation of "false realities," which then became "news events."[8]

Fear is the predominant emotion engendered by the "false realities" that become "news events." When we are afraid, we invest our resources in protection rather than growth, beginning at the physiological level. Our immune system (designed to protect us from internal threats such as viruses, bacteria and cancer cells) shuts down and our adrenal system (designed to protect us from exterior threats) goes into high gear. Moreover, we become less intelligent. Bruce Lipton writes,

> Stress hormones cause the blood vessels in the forebrain to constrict, forcing the blood to the hindbrain to nourish the high-speed reflex center used in stressful conditions. Basically, constricting the blood vessels in the forebrain shuts down consciousness and intelligence. So an interesting and unwanted aspect of the stress response is that we become less intelligent when we are under stress. Therefore, a group of people or a nation that is bathed in fear is less intelligent than a nation that is living in growth and harmony; those living in fear will make "hindbrain" reflex decisions that may be inappropriate. This may account for some of the conditions of the world we live in right now because the fear levels are so great…our biology doesn't know the difference between a real fear and a made-up fear. The simple reality is that our perceptions and beliefs, whether right or wrong, are still going to control our biology.[9]

The media's creation of false reality puts us into a trance in which we are so frightened that we forget who we are individually and as a people. Out of contact with our intelligence, we succumb to superficial sound bites, and we allow ourselves to be branded as conservatives or liberals, Republicans or Democrats, red or blue. We dissipate our energy in fighting over imagined differences, demonize the other side, forget our common humanity and lose touch with the feelings and needs that all human beings share. Even more than the political positions espoused on some talk radio and TV news shows, the message is that shouting and name-calling are the only way to communicate because the other side isn't worth listening to.

## Neither Red nor Blue

Consider the following research by the Public Policy Institute of the University of Maryland, reported by Robert F. Kennedy Jr.:

> Researchers quizzed people based upon their knowledge of current events and party affiliation. What they found is that there is not a values deficit but a huge information deficit among people who vote Republican. For example, 70 percent of the people who said they voted for George Bush believed that Saddam Hussein bombed the World Trade Center. 70 percent believe weapons of mass destruction *had* been found in Iraq. 55 percent believe that the American invasion of Iraq was strongly supported by Muslims on the street... and by our traditional allies in Europe....All that was totally wrong.
>
> The researchers went back two more times. The second time they wanted to find out where the source of misinformation came from. Invariably the people

> who had all this misinformation said their primary news source was Fox news or talk radio.
>
> They went back a third time to determine what people's essential values were. They asked a series of hypothetical questions. For example, what if there were no weapons of mass destruction in Iraq? What if Saddam Hussein had nothing to do with bombing the World Trade Center? What if the American invasion of Iraq was mostly opposed on the Muslim street and among our traditional allies in Europe? Should we have still gone in? 84 percent of Democrats and 84 percent of Republicans said the same thing. "We should not." There was no difference in values. The only difference was in information....[10]

Kennedy's point is that when we are not in a delusional trance state that separates us from one another and when we are in touch with our light, both Democrats and Republicans generally think and act in ways that are consistent with loving concern for our whole human family. Most of us want a world in which everyone has what they need.

## Where Have You Seen Through the Trance?

It can be quite frightening to realize that much of what comes to us through the mainstream media and other aspects of our culture is intended to put us into a delusional trance state. Entrancement disconnects us from our light, our power, our inner knowing...our very self. Perhaps if we can find even one small way in which we see through efforts to entrance us, that can give us confidence in our ability to reclaim ourselves in other areas as well.

For example, when I (Sheila) feel intimidated by the power of the corporate media, I think about food. I am very sensitive to the energy in created things and I intuitively know the difference between what Michael Pollan calls, "edible food-like substances"[11] and real, whole, nourishing food. In this area, I trust my inner radar. No amount of publicity from agribusiness, fast food companies, genetic modifiers such as Monsanto or anyone else can convince me that something is good for human beings to eat when I know it isn't.

If ever I do feel confused, as I sometimes have by the industrial organic food system, I ask questions and I know where to find answers. I also know where to buy eggs from pastured chickens and raw milk. I've been to the pesticide-free farm where we get most of the produce we can't grow in our own garden. Since my body does not do well on an entirely vegetarian diet, I've searched out local ranchers who raise grass-fed and grass-finished beef and lamb that are killed humanely. In this area of my life, I feel empowered and entirely in touch with my own knowing.

Whenever I feel intimidated by the power of the media, I remind myself that if I can find my own power in relation to food, I can find it in other areas as well. One way I find it is by sharing with others who see through the trance in ways I may not. I tell them about food and they tell me about what they know. For example, we have a friend who worked in the White House under two presidents and understands the difference between what actually happens at the highest levels of our government and what is reported to the public. He helps us resist entrancement, and we help him.

## Healing Process: Seeing Through the Trance

1. Close your eyes and sit comfortably with your feet flat on the floor. Place your hand on your heart and breathe deeply. Imagine that you are breathing in and out through your heart.

2. In what area of your life do you trust your own knowing? Where is your radar intact? Although you may remain open to new information, in what area of your life do you feel enough in touch with yourself that you are resistant to being conned, disempowered or entranced?
3. As you get in touch with this, notice how you feel in your body. Where do you carry your inner knowing? You may wish to move your hand to this place as a way of acknowledging and thanking this part of yourself. Let this part of you expand and fill the rest of your body.
4. Based on your ability to trust your inner radar in this area, is there another area of entrancement where you want to grow in your ability to think for yourself and trust your own knowing?
5. Is there another person or a community of people whose radar you trust and with whom you might give and receive support and encouragement?

## Chapter 8

# GRIEVING CAN HELP US TELL THE TRUTH

We recall a dinner conversation with a cousin, Joe, who is at the other end of the political spectrum from ourselves. We were discussing an issue about which we especially disagree with him. Suddenly Joe said, in reference to our country and in a voice choking with grief, "What is happening to us?!" We'll never forget the sadness in his eyes and the vulnerability on his normally rather expressionless face. As we grieved with Joe, we felt a new depth of connection with him. His perception of the problem and his solutions are not ours, but his visible grief united our hearts and moved the conversation from a political argument to shared longing for common solutions. Ever since then, when we hear political views like Joe's, much as we disagree with them, we feel compassion for the one who holds them and remember that we're all in it together.

Even when we know that something's wrong, unresolved grief can keep us from finding our voice and working for change. For example, when Michael Russell began working for the Brown Lung Association, he tried to organize mill workers to fight for legislation that would protect them from brown lung disease. He grew increasingly frustrated with the workers who, rather than planning concrete strategies for change, spent every meeting retelling stories of loved ones who had died and other ways their community had suffered from the disease.

The turning point came when workers and organizers attended a meeting with government official Eula Bingham. As she entered the room, she began to cry with frustration over the congressional session she had just left. Soon everyone in the room was crying. When the crying ended, the mill workers were, for the first time, able to speak concretely and effectively for their cause. Eula Bingham's willingness to appear weak and vulnerable, as she released her grief through tears, gave the mill workers permission to release their grief for their deceased loved ones and their own continued suffering.[a] At that meeting Michael Russell realized for the first time that corporate or *political* grief had paralyzed his people: "The resistance we find among poor people to organizing to free themselves from oppressive circumstances is the end effect of unresolved political grief."[1]

Psychotherapist Joanna Macy believes that all of us are carrying more or less buried grief for political and social situations that destroy life, such as nuclear arms, world hunger and environmental pollution. After leading many "Despair Empowerment Workshops," she concludes that by facing our grief and despair and releasing our feelings, we find new power to work for change.[2]

Our point is that bottled-up grief immobilizes us. Moreover, the more we love what we have lost and the more it represents to us, the more painful it is to face our loss and feel our grief. Yet, when we do grieve, our power to act in the very situation that pains us is released. We wonder if, as Americans, we also carry grief that is very specific to the current situation in the United States.

---

[a]Note that continually retelling a story of loss is not the same as releasing grief. Telling the same story over and over again can be a sign that the underlying feelings have not yet been expressed nor heard. When those feelings truly are expressed, heard and thereby released, the compulsion to retell the story normally disappears. For more on listening to negative feelings, see chapter 12.

## The Golden Door

Most of us grew up with a dream of America and a deep faith in the intrinsic goodness of our country. In our childhood classrooms, we began every day reciting the "Pledge of Allegiance." At baseball or football games, we listen to "The Star Spangled Banner" or "God Bless America," often with tears in our eyes. If asked why we feel grateful for our country, our list might include things like First-Amendment rights of freedom of speech, the press and religion. Almost all our ancestors risked everything to come here as immigrants, often because of religious persecution, full of hope that finally they would be safe and free. Others were trying to escape grinding poverty in countries where the "lower" classes could never be equal to the wealthy and had no hope of improving their lives.

Like many Americans' ancestors, our grandparents entered through Ellis Island, saw the Statue of Liberty and never forgot her words:

> Give me your tired, your poor,
> Your huddled masses yearning to breathe free,
> The wretched refuse of your teeming shore.
> Send these, the homeless, the tempest-tost to me.
> I lift my lamp beside the golden door.

Those who took these words seriously have urged, pestered, petitioned, harassed and demonstrated to get our country to live up to them. The result was women's suffrage, labor unions and later child-labor laws, the civil rights movement, and many other ways in which we have tried to live out our constitution's principles of democracy.

Most of us are rightly proud of our successes as a country in this regard, especially if our own families have "made it" here. My (Sheila's) immigrant grandfather sold pencils on the streets of Boston and my grandmother worked in a sewing factory for five cents an hour. She sent money back to Europe so her siblings could join her here, including her brother, Israel Nasher. His son, Raymond Nasher, was the first Jew to graduate from Duke Law School. Raymond later endowed Duke's Nasher Museum of Art. He became a delegate to the United Nations, an advisor to presidents and a prominent philanthropist. He amassed one of the finest sculpture collections in the world and founded the Nasher Sculpture Center to house it, as a gift to the City of Dallas.

When the "American Dream" works, as it did for members of my family, the danger is that "America" can easily become an overinflated symbol of salvation, in which we project onto our country our deepest longings and our highest values and ideals. It can be very painful to give this up in order to face the dark side of our country.

Moreover, love for our country can become idolatry, and patriotism can become nationalistic faith. America can be our God, and the symbols of America such as the national anthem or the flag can mean as much or more to us as religious symbols. When this happens, criticizing America may seem blasphemous. If we were to face the dark side of American history, for many of us it would be like having our faith shattered. Thus, not only do we avoid grieving for our country because painful feelings are just that—painful, and therefore easily buried; we may also avoid what needs to be grieved because we would have to disentangle God and America.[3]

Another aspect of this may be the extent to which we project our own family experience onto our country and our parents onto our government leaders. If our early experience involved abuse or other forms of oppression and we have not grieved the loss of a safe home and nurturing parents, then we may resist grieving for our country because it may require us to face unresolved grief for our own early life (see chapter 13, "Coming Out from Under the Cloud").

## Healing Process: Positive Memories of Our Country

The notion that America has a dark side may feel disturbing and painful. We can more easily face pain when we are in touch with positive memories, in this case of our country. Such memories give us strength, hope and security. In chapter 2, we emphasized the importance of doing this as individuals, beginning at the physiological level, since positive memories strengthen our immune systems. We also need to do this as a people. Remembering, for example, the words on the Statue of Liberty that greeted our ancestors is, according to Joanna Macy, like "partaking together of an excellent and wholesome meal." In order to strengthen "our cultural immune system, we need to remember who we are and the sources of our strength; memories help us do that."[4] Only when we are in touch with positive memories can we face pain and care for it with the love we have received.

(This process is oriented toward Americans. If you are a citizen of another country, we encourage you to adapt it accordingly.)

1. Sit comfortably, close your eyes, breathe deeply and place your hand on your heart. Let your awareness go down into your heart and imagine that you are breathing in and out through your heart.
2. Recall one or more moments when you felt happy and proud to be an American. What were you most grateful for? How has the United States nurtured and cared for you and your loved ones? Hold your feeling of appreciation for your country in your heart, and let it grow there.
3. As you read further, let this feeling of appreciation remind you that the dark side of America is only that—a side. It's not the whole truth any more than is the glorified image, with which many of us were raised, of a country that can do no wrong.

## What Is Happening to Us?

We recently had Christmas dinner with friends of Norwegian descent. The conversation focused on their homeland. Norway has the highest standard of living in the world. Everyone has health care and new mothers are allowed one year of paid maternity leave. Chronically ill people who cannot use the public bus system are given a car, and those whose illness is such that they cannot tolerate the long winters are sent to the tropics for two-week vacations. Police do not carry guns…some have poodles instead.

Norway has no capital punishment nor life imprisonment; the longest prison sentence is twenty-one years. Convicted criminals live on a beautiful island in small houses. They can roam the island freely and travel to the mainland to work. Wardens work alongside the prisoners, for example picking potatoes together. Prison officials believe that if people are treated decently, they will respond in kind. It appears they are right, because, despite the recent mass murder by one mentally ill person, Norway has the lowest murder rate in the world.[5b]

As we heard all this, we felt a mixture of awe, wonder and grief. What would it be like to live in such a place where human needs are met? Why can't we do that here? Immediately after September 11, 2001, we *did* do it here…temporarily. In the month

[b]As this book went to press, Norwegian Anders Breivik murdered seventy-seven people in Norway, including politicians and politically active youth. Breivik appears to be mentally ill. His actions shocked his country, where even government officials normally feel safe enough to walk the streets without security. Most significant to us is not this tragic anomaly in a country where such violence is virtually unheard of, but rather Norway's response. Instead of seeking vengeance or curtailing civil liberties, Norwegian leaders focused on maintaining freedom and democracy. At a remembrance service for the victims, the prime minister said, "We have memorials in churches and in mosques, in parliament and in the government headquarters, on the streets and in squares…Evil has brought out the best in us. Hatred engenders love." See Matthew Taylor, "Norway Prime Minister Urges Nation to 'Embrace Freedom,'" guardian.co.uk, July 29, 2011, http://www.guardian.co.uk/world/ 2011/ jul/29/norway-prime-minister-speaks-funerals (accessed September 24, 2011).

following, two-thirds of Americans shared either time or money. People waited in four-hour lines to give blood. State prison inmates in Texas, who earned an average of nineteen cents an hour for their work, raised a total of over $1,743 for the 9/11 victims.[6] The bumper sticker, "Practice random acts of kindness," proliferated. Highway toll booth workers reported that a record number of drivers were paying the toll for the car behind them. How did we get from such generosity and care for the common good to George W. Bush's, "If you want to help America, go shopping"? Instead of falling back on increasing Gross National Product (GNP) as a remedy, what if we had focused on Gross National Happiness (GHP), as they do in Bhutan?[7] What would we have done if we had stayed in touch with our best instincts as Americans?

Sadly, we didn't stay in touch with our best instincts and focus on meeting human needs rather than shopping. We shopped big time, and bought a war in Iraq that cost more than a trillion dollars. Our violence, aggression and lack of compassion have been directed not only at external "enemies," such as Iraq, but at our own people as well. For example, unlike Norway, the United States is one of the few developed countries that still has capital punishment. Only China, Iran, Pakistan, Iraq and Sudan execute more people than we do per capita.[8] Yet our murder rate is one of the highest in the developed world and our rate of incarceration, 756 per 100,000 people, is the highest in the world in comparison with 210 other countries (England, for example has 153 prisoners per 100,000 people).[9c]

---

[c]Social problems in the United States, such as high rates of incarceration and murder, are not simply a matter of losing touch with our best instincts, but also of a fundamental inequality in our economic system. There is one variable that drives the relationship between meeting human needs and alleviating violence (e.g., gun violence and homicide), as well as other social problems such as obesity, cancer, infant mortality, imprisonment ratios, depression, drug abuse, teenage pregnancies, venereal disease rates, use of prescription antidepressants, workplace satisfaction, trust of one's neighbors…ALL of them are driven by a single variable.

We work in a women's prison in Massachusetts whenever we are nearby. Most of the inmates are there because of drug-related offenses, and underneath their involvement with drugs are poverty, low self-esteem and sexual abuse. Their greatest need is for the kindness shown to those who break the law in Norway.

Most of us are not in prison, but we all experience a darkened and chilling atmosphere in the United States today, through the loss of civil liberties. Our phones have been illegally wiretapped, our e-mails have been read, and librarians have been forced to report what books we check out. Meanwhile, our corporations grow ever more powerful as they pollute our air, water and food for the sake of profit. According to the United Nations, three species die every hour because of environmental pollution.[10]

Our own species isn't doing too well, either, when it comes to toxic substances. One example is the use of aspartame (also known as Nutrasweet or Equal), monosodium glutamate (MSG) and genetically modified organisms (GMO's) in foods. These substances, present in most processed and fast foods, are known to be toxic to human beings, causing everything from brain tumors and neurological disorders to gastrointestinal problems

---

And that variable isn't wealth. While America is the richest nation in the world with a median income of around $44,000 a year, we're way in the back of the pack in all the indices mentioned above. So is the second richest nation, Great Britain.

The reason…is pretty straightforward. While most European and developed nations have a ratio of about 3:1 to 5:1 between the wealth of the poorest 20 percent of the populace and the richest 20 percent, the U.K. and U.S. are running in the neighborhood of 8:1.

The more unequal a society is, the more problems it has. Regardless of how rich it is.

"Conversely, the more equal a society is the better it does. Regardless of how poor it is (as long as they're above a baseline survival threshold, which appears to run around $5,000 a year). Costa Rica, at around $7,000 a year, does better than the U.S. or U.K. on all of the items on the list above—and more" (Thom Hartman, "The Impact of Inequality: How to Make Sick Societies Healthier" [review of Richard Wilkinson, *The Impact of Inequality: How to Make Sick Societies Healthier* (New York: New Press, 2006), www.buzzflash.com/print/9358, September 4, 2009] (accessed September 4, 2009).

and obesity. In the case of aspartame, for example, the evidence for its toxicity was in the hands of the FDA. However, a proposed ban on its use was overruled in 1985 through the political influence of Donald Rumsfeld while he was CEO of the Searle Corporation (which developed aspartame).[11]

These are only a few examples of the dark side of our country, the vast disparity between who we could be and who we are. Before we can move on, we need to grieve what we have lost.

## How Do We Grieve?

We all have reason to grieve. For example, the three of us needed to grieve for a time when we took it for granted that we and John would have a future, when we could trust the institutions of our society and when we felt proud to be Americans. Grieving means letting go of what we have lost so that we can grasp a new future.

Grieving is a natural process. Over forty years ago, Dr. Elisabeth Kübler-Ross discovered that her dying patients typically passed through five stages of grief: denial (I'm not really sick), anger (It's the doctor's fault), bargaining (I'll stop smoking if I get well), depression (Why did I ever start smoking in the first place?) and acceptance (I really am going to die and I can accept it).[12] We discovered that, since any hurt is a loss similar to a small death, we pass through these same five stages in forgiving a hurt: denial (It didn't really bother me), anger (It's their fault), bargaining (I'll forgive if they apologize), depression (It's my fault) and acceptance (I'm not grateful for what happened, but I'm grateful for the gifts that came out of it).

Kübler-Ross says that dying persons will automatically move through the five stages of dying if they feel loved in the midst of whatever they are feeling. This need is normally met by having a significant other with whom they can share their feelings. We have found that the same is true of the five stages of forgiveness. The feelings at each stage are important because they put us in touch with our needs. As we meet those needs, the loss represented by the hurt is resolved. Thus, the healing process below invites us to get in touch with feelings, let ourselves be loved in the midst of them and allow our feelings to reveal our needs.[d]

This process focuses on the first stage, of denial, in which we don't want to face our loss. Denial can serve us at times when too much is coming at us and we are not in touch with sufficient resources of love to be able to face it all just yet. Denial can also lead us to tell ourselves everything is ok when we know it isn't, distract ourselves by falling back into our favorite addiction or find some other way to avoid the pain we feel. If we Americans watch ourselves as a people, it seems we are very adept at denial. Perhaps a place to begin in healing ourselves and our country is to face our denial and own the losses we grieve.

## Healing Process

(Again, this process is oriented toward Americans. If you are a citizen of another country, we encourage you to adapt it accordingly.)

1. Sit comfortably, close your eyes, breathe deeply and place your hand on your heart. Let your awareness go down into your heart and imagine that you are breathing in and out through your heart.
2. Go back to the moment(s) you got in touch with earlier, when you felt happy and proud to be an American. What were you most grateful for? How has the United States nurtured and

[d]For the entire five-stage process, see Matthew and Dennis Linn, *Healing Life's Hurts: Healing Memories through the Five Stages of Forgiveness* (New York/Mahwah, NJ: Paulist Press, 1978), and Dennis Linn, Sheila Fabricant Linn and Matthew Linn, *Don't Forgive Too Soon: Extending the Two Hands that Heal* (New York/Mahwah, NJ: Paulist Press, 1997).

cared for you and your loved ones? Hold your feeling of appreciation for your country in your heart and let it grow there.

3. Now ask yourself, what are you not so grateful for in the United States today? If you could change anything in your country, what would it be? Is there anything about being an American today that you would not want to pass on to the next generation? What have you lost about your country that you once cherished?
4. Where do you most feel that loss in your body? Place your hand there and gently care for that part of yourself.
5. Notice whatever feelings come up, and be with them without trying to fix or change them in any way.
6. What needs were once met by your country (or your image of your country)? Is there any other way those needs could be met?

## Chapter 9

# JESUS WAS UP AGAINST THE SAME THING

Imagine yourself living in a world where everyone has what they need. Such a world was Jesus' dream, and he left us a revolutionary prayer for his dream to come true: the "Lord's Prayer" (or the "Our Father").[1]

The context for the Lord's Prayer is that Jesus and the majority of his people were among the twelve million slaves of the Roman Empire.[2] With little food, enormous debts and deprived of their land, the people of Israel were constantly rebelling. For example, at about the time Jesus was born, the Roman ruler, King Herod the Great, was dying. The Jews, thinking it was their chance to throw off slavery, headed for the temple. (In Jerusalem the biggest homes belonged to the Roman rulers and to the high priests of the temple, who were appointed by the Romans and behaved as their puppets.) Once at the temple, the Jews took down an image of an eagle, the symbol of Roman occupation. However, this rebellion didn't last long.[3]

In retaliation, Herod's son, Archelaus, organized three Roman legions. They killed or enslaved tens of thousands, including two thousand Jewish freedom fighters whom they hung from crosses.[4] One of the largest towns, Sepphoris (with a population of twelve thousand), was four kilometers from Nazareth. The Romans burned Sepphoris and killed or enslaved all of the inhabitants.[5]

Jesus almost certainly lost members of his extended family there. He may have even worked on the reconstruction of the city, which involved carpenters, masons and other laborers from villages within a thirty-mile radius.[6] Later as an adult, Jesus would continue the struggle for Jewish rights as he confronted the Romans and the temple establishment. For his efforts, he would ultimately receive the same punishment as thousands of other Jews: being hung from a cross.[7]

The Lord's Prayer is part of Jesus' confrontation of the Roman system. When it asks that God's "kingdom come on earth as it is in heaven," the prayer is pleading that the loving mystery that underpins the universe—not Caesar, nor the high priests, nor the landowners, nor the banks and corporations in our time—be in charge of human life. What would human life look like if the mystery we call God were in charge?[8]

First, everyone would have enough to eat. "Give us this day our daily bread," was the plea of most Jews, since under Roman domination much of the grain grown in the slave colonies (400,000 tons annually) was shipped directly to Rome. Left with just the crumbs to eat, the price of food skyrocketed beyond what most could afford. Perhaps this is why so much of Jesus' life centered on bread, from the parables that encourage us to invite everyone to the table to his many feedings of the hungry crowds.[9]

In fact, when Christians wanted to remember Jesus and to live in his spirit, they gathered in communities where they broke and shared their bread with one another. In such communities, "There was not a needy person among them" (Acts 4:34). To share food was a subversive act that said, "We are not willing to wait for the crumbs that the Romans see fit to give us."[10]

However, for many of those who wanted to share food with one another, because of the exorbitant prices it meant they would ultimately end up at the moneylender's (also controlled by Roman supporters), where interest rates ranged from 25 to 250 percent. These interest rates together with high taxes forced many Jews into homelessness as they lost their land through foreclosures.

Although it is true that in the Acts community "no one was in need," the same verse tells us why: "…for as many who owned fields or houses sold them" (Acts 4:34). Eventually, in Galilee where Jesus lived, so many had been forced to sell their land in order to eat that three families owned 60 percent of the land.[11]

The plea of the Lord's Prayer, which we often translate as "Forgive us our trespasses as we forgive those who trespass against us," is probably more accurately translated, "Forgive us our debts as we forgive our debtors."[12] In Luke 4:16–20, where Jesus declares the purpose of his life, he emphasizes that one of his main purposes is debt forgiveness or "to proclaim the year of the Lord's favor." This Jubilee (Lev 25—26, Deut 15), thought by the prophets (Ezek 18, Jer 34, Neh 5) to be a "nonnegotiable" of the Bible, assured that everyone would get what they needed through the periodic forgiveness of all debts, release of those enslaved because of debts, and return to the original owners of land lost because of debt.

In Luke 4, when Jesus speaks of the purpose of his life, he quotes word for word a Jubilee text from the prophet Isaiah (61:1–2), except that Jesus changes the last phrase of Isaiah, "a day of vengeance of our God," to "a year of the Lord's favor." Whereas the text from Isaiah proclaims the Jubilee year only for the Jews and encourages punishment for all their enemies, Jesus proclaims an end to punishment and an extension of the rules of the Jubilee year to all nations. The proponents of the vengeance tradition, who wanted punishment for the Sidonians, Romans and Syrians, were so angered that they wanted to hurl Jesus off the mountain. By extending the Jubilee year to all nations, Jesus wanted to emphasize that not only would the Jews have their material needs met, but so would everyone else.[13]

Besides the Lord's Prayer, many of the other sayings and parables of Jesus, such as the parable of the workers discussed in chapter 6, describe his dream for humanity. For example, in the parable of the workers there are no debts; the workers who arrived late are not told, "You still owe me more hours of work." And everyone receives their daily bread, symbolized by the living wage of one denarius.

## A Story of Conscientious Objection: The Parable of the Pounds

Perhaps the parable that best describes how Jesus nonviolently confronted the Roman and temple establishment in his quest to assure that everyone would have what they need is the parable of the pounds in Luke 19:11–27, often identified with the parable of the talents in Matthew 25:14–30. This is the story of a nobleman who goes away to be crowned king. He gives each of his servants a pound and asks them to multiply this money while he is gone. The people hated him so much that they sent a delegation after him, trying to stop his coronation. He was crowned anyway and when he returned, he summoned his slaves and asked how much they had earned with his money.

> The first came forward and said, "Lord, your pound has made ten more pounds." He said to him, "Well done, good slave! Because you have been trustworthy in a very small thing, take charge of ten cities." Then the second came, saying, "Lord, your pound has made five pounds." He said to him, "And you, rule over five cities." Then the other came, saying, "Lord, here is your pound. I wrapped it up in a piece of cloth, for I was afraid of you, because you are a harsh man; you take what you did not deposit, and reap what you did not sow." He said to him, "I will judge you by your own words, you wicked slave! You knew, did you, that I was a harsh man, taking what I did not deposit and

> reaping what I did not sow? Why then did you not put my money into the bank? Then when I returned, I could have collected it with interest." He said to the bystanders, "Take the pound from him and give it to the one who has ten pounds." (And they said to him, "Lord, he has ten pounds!") "I tell you, to all those who have, more will be given; but from those who have nothing, even what they have will be taken away. But as for these enemies of mine who did not want me to be king over them—bring them here and slaughter them in my presence."

If we act out this parable at a retreat and ask which servant was the hero of the story, most people respond, "The servant that brought back ten pounds." When asked if they like the man of noble birth, people usually say, "No." Some don't like him because he is a murderer, others because he steals from the poor and gives to the rich, others because he is vengeful and hard-hearted. In Mexico, when we asked our audience if they liked him, they shouted, "No! He is like our government!"

If we didn't already know the nobleman was a tyrant, a clue (that Americans might miss) is that he wanted his money invested in order to earn interest. Jews called the practice of charging interest "usury." They knew that such a practice led to the loss of homes and land, and in Jesus' time the Jewish community's list of the seven most despised professions included usury.[14] Usurers were denied all civil and religious rights. Usury was not only denounced by Jesus but, even as late as 1569, three papal bulls unequivocally condemned it.

What (and whom), then, is this parable about? *The Jerusalem Bible* footnote for this passage suggests one possible explanation.[15] According to the footnote, the cruel nobleman probably represents Archelaus. After the death of his father, Herod the Great in 4 BC,

Archelaus went to Rome to receive his inheritance. There, he was crowned ruler of Judea. On his return from Rome, the hated Archelaus put to death a delegation of fifty Jews who had tried to block him from being confirmed as ruler. (In Matthew 2:22, even Mary and Joseph, as they returned from Egypt, were warned in a dream not to return to Archelaus's Judean territory.) Archelaus committed so many atrocities that in AD 6, Caesar Augustus deposed him for fear the Jews would riot.

The hero, then, is the servant who, even though it will cost him his life, becomes a conscientious objector. He buries Archelaus's coin rather than investing it to earn more money for the coffers that supported Archelaus's tyranny. The other servants all become part of the ruler's repressive government as they receive cities to oversee.

Jesus tells this parable just before mounting his donkey (not a warhorse) on his way to Jerusalem. Once in Jerusalem, he confronts the temple establishment, which ultimately leads to his crucifixion (Luke 19:45–48). As a resister to both the religious and political domination system, he is charged with wanting to destroy the temple and make himself a king. The parable's servant who is a conscientious objector represents Jesus and how he, too, is sentenced to death by the domination system that he constantly resisted.

This system, according to Walter Wink, is characterized by

> ...patriarchal gender relations, autocratic power relations, inequitable economic relations, class caste ranking and hierarchical social relations—with the whole edifice defended and preserved by a belief in redemptive violence...the message of Jesus was a specific repudiation of this system of domination which had, by his day, metastasized throughout virtually the entire known world. The gospel Jesus proclaimed was a disease-specific remedy for the evils of this Domination System.[16]

Thus, one possible interpretation of the parable of the pounds is that Jesus is inviting us to join him as conscientious objectors in confronting and resisting the domination system of our own world at all costs.[17][a]

How many of us have ever heard an interpretation of the parable of the pounds where the emphasis has been on using our gifts or talents well? In such interpretations we are told that we will be rewarded if we use our gifts and serve generously, just as the nobleman rewarded the servant who returned with ten pounds. However, we will be punished if we hide our gifts. Such an interpretation is religion colluding with the domination system. It presents the mystery we call God as no better than the nobleman whom everyone hates. And most importantly, it misses the revolutionary stance of the Lord's Prayer, where Jesus is trying to awaken his listeners to the possibility of living in a world where there are no rewards or punishments and where everyone's needs are met.

In other words, Jesus was up against the same thing as many of us are today. How can we live in the world of musical chairs where everyone wins, instead of a world of domination where there are a few winners and a whole lot of losers? Although Jesus

---

[a]The world Jesus dreamed of and died for did exist for thousands of years before he was born. According to cultural historian Riane Eisler, between about 7,000 BC and 3,500 BC, peaceful societies flourished in the Near East and what is now Europe. These societies were based upon partnership, in which men and women were equals. Equality and cooperation between the two fundamental halves of humanity were reflected throughout these societies and in their relationships with their neighbors. There was an absence of war and, aside from basic survival, the emphasis was upon peace, creativity and enjoying life. Resources were relatively evenly distributed, rather than the wealthy few exploiting masses of the poor. Power meant the ability to empower others and actualize possibilities, not the ability to dominate others. The image of the divine was of a mother giving birth to a child. See Riane Eisler, *The Chalice and the Blade* (New York: HarperCollins, 1988); *Tomorrow's Children* (Boulder, CO: Westview Press, 2000). As mentioned earlier, human society based upon peace, cooperation and mutuality may have existed for far more than the few thousand years identified by Eisler. This way of life was likely the norm during most of the seven million–year history of our human and protohuman ancestors. See O'Murchu, *Ancestral Grace.*

did not have the modern media to contend with, his people were nonetheless entranced in their own way. A combination of military violence and religious legalism convinced most of them that the Roman system of slavery, poverty, tyranny and fear-based religion in which they lived was the only possible reality. Through his teachings and the example of his life, Jesus followed in the footsteps of many great leaders who knew there is another way to live.

## Speaking in Parables

If Jesus really objected so much to the religious, political and economic system of his time, wouldn't he just have said so more directly? If it is true that Jesus was a conscientious objector, then we can better understand why he spoke in parables.

Several years ago, we (Matt and Denny) went to Korea shortly after the Kyongju massacre in which the Korean military murdered as many as twenty thousand government protesters. Our sponsors asked us to travel to the major cities, including Kyongju, to help people heal this hurt. Wherever we went, the Korean police followed us. They wanted to make sure we never mentioned the Kyongju massacre. If we had, they would have arrested us and our sponsors.

So, we spent two weeks speaking in parables. For example, Matt would speak about the five stages of forgiveness that he had gone through in forgiving a student who attacked him. Then we would lead people through a process to forgive someone who had hurt them. Tens of thousands of people attended those conferences. Most wept as they began the process of healing the hurt caused by the Kyongju massacre, despite the fact that we never once mentioned the massacre itself.

Like ourselves in Korea, Jesus was also watched. In order to survive and still confront the domination system of his time, he, too, often had to speak in parables. In his parables and in the

Lord's Prayer, Jesus dreamed of a world in which everyone's needs would be met. In order to realize his dream, he had to first be honest about the world as it was in his time.

## Healing Process: Finding the Strength to Resist Injustice

1. Close your eyes, sit comfortably and breathe deeply. Put your hand on your heart and imagine that you are breathing in and out through your heart.
2. Recall a time when you refused to cooperate with injustice—a time when you were a conscientious objector and nonviolently resisted injustice toward yourself or another.
3. Relive that moment and notice how you feel inside your body. Hold that energy in your heart and let it grow there.
4. Is there any area of your present life in which you need that same energy, for example, a current situation of injustice or abuse toward yourself or another that you want to resist?

## Chapter 10

# HEALING OUR DIMINISHED SENSE OF SELF

Have you ever felt overwhelmed by the enormity of the problems facing us? The sense that we are in a period of extreme crisis is widespread. What gives us hope is the equally widespread awareness of an unprecedented shift in consciousness. This shift might be summarized as a growing recognition that all creation is one whole, interconnected, unified field.

Musical chairs is our image for it. The traditional way of playing divides us into winners and losers, a division that belies our essential unity. When we change the rules and play cooperatively, everyone wins. The nonviolent movements for human and civil rights of recent decades, the cultural creatives mentioned in chapter 3 and Paul Hawken's list of one to two million grassroots groups based on cooperative values are all part of this shift.

The transition from a world of division to one of unity is not easy, because we've grown so accustomed to the domination system and the competition it engenders. Change of this magnitude is scary. Not only are many of us afraid of what we see in our present world, but we are also afraid of an unknown future. One of the main symptoms of anxiety and fear is physical and emotional constriction. We may experience ourselves as trapped and without possibilities.

For example, during our months of being in a PTSD-like state, we (Denny and Sheila) could not dream of the future. Our breathing was shallow, we felt dread rather than hope and our focus was on survival rather than expansion. When a retreat invitation came, our first impulse was to say, "No," rather than imagining the new presentations we might create or the new people we might meet.

How can we and our families live in a wholesome, peaceful and loving way during this time? How can we find our voices and expand into our full human potential, rather than allowing fear of the future to constrict us?

## How Big Are We?

We've probably all heard about how we only use 5 to 10 percent of our brain. We usually think this means that if we just tried harder, we could memorize ten times more information to help us figure out how to invent ten times more technologies, to manipulate ten times more of the material world. Educator Joseph Chilton Pearce suggests that our brains are so powerful that it *only takes* 5 to 10 percent of our brain to memorize all the information we need to invent all the possible technologies we could ever use. According to him, we don't use the other 90 to 95 percent of our brain because it's intended for something different—it's intended for expanded consciousness, for things that transcend space and time.[1]

Few of us can imagine how large and vast we really are. Since we tend to regard ourselves as superior to animals and other creatures, perhaps we can begin with them. Scientist Rupert Sheldrake has done extensive studies of the "unexplained powers of animals."[2] One of his research studies involves N'kisi, an African gray parrot who lives in Harlem with his caregiver, Aimee. N'kisi intelligently uses a vocabulary of over 950 words and demonstrates a sense of humor. When N'kisi met Jane Goodall, whom he had seen in pictures with apes, N'kisi immediately recognized her and asked, "Got a chimp?" When another parrot hung upside down on his perch, N'kisi said, "You got to put this bird on the camera." He invents words and phrases to describe things that are new to him, just as human children do. For example, N'kisi's name for the flower essences used by Aimee (an aromatherapist) is "pretty smell medicine."[3]

N'kisi can also express Aimee's unspoken thoughts, feelings and dreams. For example, at the exact moment when Aimee was dreaming of pressing the button of a tape recorder, N'kisi woke her by saying, "Press the button." N'kisi is able to read Aimee's thoughts even when she is not physically present.[4]

Dr. Sheldrake also has many research studies and over 800 anecdotal accounts involving dogs whose behavior changed visibly (e.g., looking out the window or sitting by the door) at the moment their human guardian formed the intention to return home. This happened even when the guardian was thousands of miles away.[5]

Dr. Sheldrake has 359 accounts of similar behavior in cats.[6] In his survey of all sixty-five animal clinics in northern London, every one reported that cats commonly are nowhere to be found at the exact time when their guardians are ready to take them to an appointment with the veterinarian. This became such a problem that one clinic stopped scheduling appointments and encouraged guardians to simply bring the cat whenever they could.[7]

The behavior of many dogs and cats changes when their guardian is calling on the telephone. Some cats are so upset if no one picks up the receiver that they will desperately try to pick it up themselves.[8]

Dr. Sheldrake insists that these capacities are not only normal for animals, but for us "superior" humans as well. For example, have you ever had the telephone ring and, before you answered, known who was calling? Have you ever sensed that someone you loved had just died and discovered later that they did die at exactly that moment? Have you ever been pregnant and experienced your baby coming to you in a dream to tell you that it was a boy or a girl?

Many of these common human experiences, such as knowing who is calling, have been carefully researched. Eighty percent of the population have experienced "telephone telepathy," and in various studies of this, subjects could correctly identify which of four people was calling them on the phone at least 42 percent of the time (rather than the 25 percent we might expect). The odds of this happening by chance are one in one trillion.[9] In a study at Johns Hopkins University of pregnant women who dreamed of their baby's sex, the mothers were correct 100 percent of the time.[10]

How do you feel when you hear such things? We notice a feeling of awe within ourselves...awe *at* ourselves and at the untapped, vast potential of our human consciousness. How do we access this potential? How can we live in such a way that our sense of self is true to size, rather than accept the diminishment and frustration that is so common in our culture?

## Appreciation and Love Are the Doorway

One answer comes from research at the Institute of HeartMath on the power of feelings of appreciation and love. As we mentioned earlier, when we hold such feelings in our heart for even a few seconds, our heart rate becomes coherent (ordered, harmonious and efficient). Because the heart has the strongest electrical field of any bodily system, a coherent heart rate in turn pulls or entrains our brain and other bodily systems into a state of coherence.

The concept of entrainment comes from observations of pendulums. If two or more clocks whose pendulums are swinging differently are placed side by side on the same platform,[11] the one with the strongest rhythm will pull the others into sync with it so that eventually all the pendulums are swinging in unison. Similarly, the heart, which is the "strongest biological oscillator in the human system,"[12] pulls all the other bodily systems into entrainment with its rhythm. According to HeartMath scientists,

> ...when we're in a state of deep love or appreciation, the brain synchronizes—comes into harmony—with the heart's harmonious rhythms....This state of head/heart entrainment occurs precisely when the heart rhythms complete one cycle every ten seconds (0.1 Hz).
>
> When brain waves entrain with heart rhythms at 0.1Hz, subjects in our studies report heightened intuitive clarity and a greater sense of well-being....
>
> According to our studies, at those elusive moments when we transcend our ordinary performance and feel in harmony with something else—whether it's a glorious sunset, inspiring music or another human being—what we're really coming into sync with is ourselves....In entrainment, we're at our optimal functioning capacity.
>
> Our research shows that people can develop their ability to maintain entrainment by sustaining sincere, heart-focused states such as appreciation and love.[13]

The HeartMath research on appreciation and love can help us understand why it is not every dog that goes to the door when its master forms the intention to return home, nor every parrot that reads the thoughts of its owner, nor every cat that answers the phone. A pet is more likely to do such things the more love and appreciation it receives from its owner. So, too, it is not every caller that can guess correctly when the phone rings. Our ability to do this increases to the extent we feel love and appreciation for the person who is calling, which may be why success is highest with best friends followed by mothers and spouses.[14] Thus love and appreciation can open us to the vastness of who we are and to the vastness of the created universe we encounter each day.

## Transcending Time and Space

One aspect of our vastness is our capacity to transcend time and space. Consciousness is inherently nonlocal, meaning that it is not limited by the present moment (it transcends time) nor by our physical location (it transcends space). Our mind cannot be limited to specific points in time (the present moment) nor to specific points in space (our brain). Rather, studies at reputable scientific institutions are demonstrating that our minds transcend time and space. For example,

> For about a decade, studies done at Princeton University's Engineering Anomalies Research Laboratory have indicated that subjects can influence the outcome of random physical events and can mentally convey complex information to other subjects from whom they are widely separated, even by global distances. These studies show not only that a sender can mentally transmit detailed information to a receiver on the other side of the earth, but also that the receiver usually "gets" the information up to three days before it is sent.[15]

How is this possible? A clue comes from the fact that the people who score the best at mentally transmitting information across time and space, also score the best on love, empathy and compassion.[16] So, the most loving people are those who are likely to have most developed their capacity to mentally transcend time and space.

We (Denny and Matt) experienced how love and compassion help us transcend time and space during the first retreat we gave, in Dallas. Many of the participants were in second marriages, including seven people who had not heard from their first spouse for many years and didn't even know where that spouse lived. These seven people devoted the retreat to praying for their former spouse, with an emphasis on gratefully appreciating how that person had gifted them.

When we returned to Dallas a year later, we met with the same seven people. Five of them told us that their former spouse had taken the initiative to contact them within a short time after the retreat. Some of their former spouses wrote letters, others called and one traveled 2,000 miles to seek reconciliation. We have often found in our workshops that love touches and heals hearts across time and space.

As in Dallas, one common way to transcend time and space is through prayer and meditation. For example, simply by becoming quiet and paying attention to our breathing, we can enter a state that is outside of time and space. Perhaps that is why, according to Deepak Chopra,

> Studies have shown that the longer people have been practicing meditation, the younger they score on tests of biological age. For example, long-term meditators show biological ages almost twelve years younger than their chronological age. Other studies have shown that certain hormonal changes usually associated with aging can be slowed or reversed through regular meditation.[17]

It may be that meditation reverses the aging process in part because it normally encourages a state of appreciation and love, which leads to a coherent heart rate, which in turn increases levels of the anti-aging hormone DHEA.[18] It may be that our genes have been altered, as discussed in chapter 2. It may also be that meditation reverses aging because it helps us access a state of higher consciousness in which we transcend time and space.

The physiological basis for this is that meditation diminishes lateralization in the brain. In lateralization, we access the two brain hemispheres in an imbalanced and disconnected way, and so we tend to perceive reality as separate and disconnected. However, as lateralization diminishes (which happens through meditation) and we access the two hemispheres in a more balanced way, our sense of separation diminishes and we experience ourselves as connected to all things in a way that transcends time and space.[19]

Consistent with the possibility that consciousness itself has the power to transcend the biological aging process, Dr. Chopra proposes something quite startling. He suggests that, while in a meditative state, we choose an age within the past fifteen years that we would like to be in biological terms. In effect, he is inviting us to choose an age about which we have positive, grateful memories—an age whose physical and mental capacities we would like to have now. If we do this five times per day for several days, we will begin to think and act as a person of that age and our biology will begin to reflect this.[20]

Harvard psychologist Ellen Langer demonstrated something similar in an experiment with groups of men in their seventies and eighties:

> She encouraged them to think and behave as if they were twenty years younger. After doing this for only five days, these men showed a number of physical changes associated with age reversal. Their hearing and vision improved, they performed better on tests of manual dexterity, and had improved joint mobility.[21]

As Dr. Langer's research shows, we don't need to be meditators to live in a realm that is outside time and space. There are many ways to access this realm. One of the most obvious seems to be through everyday experiences for which we feel appreciation and gratitude. If we were to write down the moments in any given day that we appreciate most, we would probably notice that those were also the moments during that day when time seemed to "fly by." For example, at the end of a day I (Sheila) am often most grateful for the time I spent cooking for guests. Most likely I was so immersed in it that the doorbell rang when I thought I still had at least another hour before our friends would arrive.

Because, like meditation, appreciation and gratitude seem to place us outside time and space, it follows that these attitudes also make our bodies younger. In a Yale University study of 660 Ohio residents, researchers discovered that people who had a positive attitude about getting old actually extended their life-span by an average of seven and a half years. In fact, this attitude of gratitude was twice as significant as any other factors related to aging, such as blood pressure, cholesterol, history of smoking, frequency of exercise, etcetera.[22]

It seems that love, appreciation and gratitude help us entrain or align our hearts and minds with the loving, creative energy—the mystery we call God—that permeates the entire universe and is constantly renewing it. This creative energy is capable of far more than keeping us young or helping us know who is calling on the telephone.

## Consciousness Is Prior to Matter

When we are aligned with loving, creative energy, we can have a positive effect on any situation in the physical world. This is true because the creative energy that can be called *spirit* or *consciousness* is prior to matter. Until around 1600, the cosmos was viewed holistically, and human souls were seen as an expression of a divine reality. Then, as a result of the scientific revolution in the seventeenth century, the worldview of Europe changed. Spirit and matter were now seen as separate, and life came to be viewed as a kind of evolutionary accident. The world—including the biological world, so including us—was now understood in a mechanistic, materialistic way, as a kind of a machine. Then the problem was to understand how consciousness could have developed in such a world. If consciousness is a "mere by-product of matter," how did it emerge from matter? No one could really answer that.[23]

Today, scientists are increasingly recognizing that it's just the opposite, that spirit or consciousness is prior to matter. A major change in worldview is underway, "...from consciousness as merely an impotent by-product of complex matter to consciousness as both fundamental and causal throughout evolution."[24] Owen Barfield describes consciousness as

> ...the inner side of the whole, just as human consciousness is the inside of one human being....Once you have realized that there is indeed only one world, though with both an inside and an outside to it, only one world experienced by our senses from without, and by our consciousness from within, it is no longer plausible to fantasize an immemorial single-track evolution of the outside world alone.[25]

From the prokaryotes (single-celled organisms) who, billions of years ago, "responded to drastic changes in their environment in ways that imply something like creative problem-solving," to dogs that know when their owners are coming home, to humans who can give and receive love and forgiveness across space and time, we all participate in "a universal process through which spirit contemplates and directs its own evolution."[26]

Instead of consciousness somehow evolving out of matter, matter is an expression of consciousness.[27] The implications are vast. For example, in the case of death, which our culture fears so much, physical dying and decay have no ultimate significance because "our essence couldn't nonexist even if we wanted it to."[28] As Teilhard de Chardin said, "Right at its base, the living world is constituted by consciousness clothed in flesh and bone."[29]

This means that the problems, illnesses and physical limitations of the material world we see around us and that we experience in our own lives are not the last word. It means that our power of love and intention can affect those circumstances to a far greater extent than we realize.

## Consciousness and Energy Signals

Another way to understand the role of spirit or consciousness in the physical world comes from cellular biology. Cells respond to all kinds of signals, for example, chemical signals like the ones in a drug or medicine, as well as energy signals. British scientist C. W. F. McClare found that energy signals are about a hundred times more effective in conveying information to cells than are chemical signals.[30] Perhaps this is because our cells are fundamentally energetic realities rather than chemical ones. Lynne McTaggart writes,

> At our most elemental, we are not a chemical reaction, but an energetic charge. Human beings and all living beings are a coalescence of energy in a field of energy connected to every other thing in the world. The pulsating energy field is the central engine of our being and our consciousness, the alpha and the omega of our existence. There is no "me" and "not-me" duality to our bodies in relation to the universe, but one underlying energy field.[31]

Prayer, love, appreciation, intention, positive thoughts, negative thoughts and so forth are all forms of energy signals, and they directly affect our cells (including our genes, as discussed in chapter 2).[32] This can be demonstrated using applied kinesiology, popularly known as *muscle testing*. Applied kinesiology is based on research at Johns Hopkins University in the 1940s and was later developed by Dr. George Goodheart.

Imagine that you extend your arm and resist any pressure while another person pushes downward on your wrist. If your body is functioning optimally, your arm will instantly lock in place, feel strong and resist going down. If your body is not functioning optimally, your arm will not lock in place and your arm will go down easily. Note that this is not a test of physical strength, but rather of whether the muscles are "turned on" or "turned off" by the nervous system. A trained practitioner who is familiar with the mechanical and energetic systems of the body can use muscle testing to evaluate many aspects of health.[33]

Muscle testing can also be used to illustrate the effect of energy signals on the body. Imagine once again that you extend your arm, this time while thinking of a person with whom you have a happy, loving relationship. Assuming your body is otherwise functioning normally (and assuming you are well hydrated, since water conducts electrical energy), if another person pushes downward on your wrist, your arm will lock in place and resist going down. With your arm still extended, if you now think of a person with whom you have a difficult and stressful relationship, your arm will feel weak and will not be able to resist the downward pressure. In other words, your positive or negative thoughts directly affect your cells sufficiently to cause an obvious change in your body.

We see something similar in the well-documented placebo effect. This is the widely observed phenomenon in which people who receive an inert or even harmful substance that they believe is an effective medication do in fact experience physical improvement. For example, when given a placebo, from 30 to 70 percent of people experience relief from pain, high blood pressure, coughs, asthma, Parkinson's disease and even baldness. Asthmatics who were given an inhaler containing salt water and told it contained an irritant couldn't breathe. When they were given the same inhaler containing salt water, but told it was medicine, their breathing capacity doubled. Even the size and quantity of pills influences their effect. People who are given a large pill notice more improvement than those given a small one containing the same amount of medicine, presumably because they believe that bigger means more powerful.[34]

Drug companies are well aware of extensive scientific research on the placebo effect and profit greatly from it. The mountain of cough medicines sold in the United States is a monument to the placebo effect, since "Recent studies have shown that cough medicines are no more effective than placebos in children and adults," and many groups such as the American Academy of Pediatrics advise against using them.[35] Even surgery can be a placebo. Some physicians are rejecting profitable arthroscopic surgery because, although patients improve, they do so at the same rate as those given sham, placebo surgery.[36]

Our thoughts create a field that not only affects our bodies, as in the placebo effect, but it also extends beyond our bodies, and this field can actually be measured through magnetoencephalography. This is different from electroencephalography, in which electrodes are placed on the skull and they physically pick up an electric current from the brain. In magnetoencephalography, the measuring device is not touching the skull at all and it picks up the magnetic field of our thoughts. In other words, our thoughts are not contained inside our head. Rather, they extend out from us in a field, and they affect everything around us. The fields of other people's thoughts affect us, as well.[37]

These fields are all entangled with each other. If enough people are producing similar fields because they're thinking similar thoughts, that creates the *crowd effect*, in which a group of people whose thoughts are coherent can have a measurable effect on events in the world.[38] It seems that quantum mechanics is confirming the traditional idea that remarkable things can happen "where two or three are gathered together" (Matt 18:20).

A striking example of this is the New York Lottery on September 11, 2002. What number do you think was on many people's minds in New York that day? The numbers drawn in the New York Lottery that evening were 9-1-1.[39] Our thoughts affect the reality around us, within our own bodies as in the placebo effect, and in the outer world as in the New York State Lottery.

## We Are Never Helpless

In our culture, perhaps what most diminishes us is a feeling of helplessness to affect the destructive forces of violence, war, poverty and injustice that seem so pervasive. Such helplessness makes us vulnerable to entrancement and manipulation by political leaders, corporate greed and the mass media. But in fact, we are never helpless in any situation. When we are in touch with love, appreciation and positive intention, we have the power to change the world.

An example of this is the village of Le Chambon in Southern France. During World War II, five thousand people lived there. They were Protestants; their pastor was André Trocme, a committed pacifist who taught his people nonviolence. Under Pastor Trocme's leadership, the people of Le Chambon took in five thousand Jews and hid them from the Nazis throughout the war. Not a single villager betrayed the Jews to the Nazis. Most remarkable of all, the Nazis knew that Jews were being hidden in Le Chambon and they did not stop it.[40] We wonder if the loving, peaceful intentions of these simple villagers created a field of goodness that protected them and their guests from even the Nazis.[a]

## Healing the Future Through the Imagination

Both positive intention and imagination are forms of energetic signals. When we imagine the world we desire, we help create it. For example, physicist John Hagelin has studied the relationship between quantum physics and higher states of consciousness. In 1993, he designed an experiment to see if the crime rate in Washington, DC, could be reduced through meditation.

Crime can be predicted quite accurately three months in advance, by considering factors such as previous crime rate, temperature, day of the week, etcetera. Hagelin proposed to lower the predicted crime rate by at least 20 percent. He received a six-million-dollar grant for his experiment and used much of it to bring four thousand experienced meditators from eighty different countries to Washington. During a two-month period, they meditated regularly with the intention that stress and other factors contributing to crime be lowered. In fact, the crime rate diminished by 25 percent. The odds of this being due to chance were less than one in one billion. An independent review board of twenty-seven sociologists, criminologists and various other experts verified these results.

During the war in Yugoslavia, Hagelin met with representatives of our National Security Council to say, in effect, "There *is*

---

[a]Perhaps the following can help us understand what happened in Le Chambon: "Studies suggest that more coherent energy influences the less coherent, that higher order influences the lower...perhaps higher stages of consciousness—as powerful morphogenic fields that act as an attractor—can encourage lower stages to evolve more quickly. The phenomena of entrainment and resonance suggest that the more we vibrate at the same frequency, the stronger the field will become, the stronger the attraction will become, and the greater ease with which the field may be entered. Intentions held by small but pulsating groups can change energy patterns all over the globe. This is an awesome power, one we must not engage frivolously" (Judy Cannato, *Field of Compassion* [Notre Dame, IN: Sorin, 2010], 158).

another way to handle this besides dropping bombs on Belgrade." He reports that people in our government were well aware of the power of intention to affect world events, but at the time the vested interests in military solutions were already too great to be stopped.[41]

## Imagination and Addictions

Imagination can help heal personal struggles as well as social ones. Treatment centers for addictions understand this. In the past, only 10 percent of clients at these centers were able to stay sober after treatment. The success rate went up to 50 percent when therapists like Mark Mitchell began using the power of the imagination. Before an alcoholic left treatment, Mark would ask, "If you imagine the scenes where you will be most tempted to drink again, how do you see yourself reacting?" If the person was not able to imagine staying sober and contented in each scene, he or she needed more treatment.

When the alcoholic seemed finally ready to be released, Mark asked a final question: "If you imagine yourself having had a drink, what do you imagine happening next?" If the alcoholic could not speak with enthusiasm about calling a sponsor, going to meetings and continuing happy and sober, that person was not yet well enough to leave. "Unless an individual can *see* himself or herself sober, he or she can't stay sober."[42] The imagination literally forms our future.

## Imagining Things That Seem Impossible

As we explored in chapter 9, Jesus imagined a world in which everyone had what they needed. Sometimes we get a glimpse of this in our world. For example, we (Denny and Sheila) have a close friend who contracted a serious illness a few years ago. We knew of something that would help him, but it would cost $3,000, which seemed impossible for us. Finally, we were so worried about him that we decided to take the money from our savings. A few minutes later, Denny was studying some government forms and realized we didn't have to pay a tax he had thought we had to pay. One hour later, we went to the mailbox and found three letters from the Internal Revenue Service telling us about refunds we hadn't expected. The total of all this was $3,000.

Have you ever had a similar experience, in which you gave something away and it came back to you? Have you ever had an experience in which you needed something that seemed beyond your reach, and there it was before you? Have you ever wanted to do something that seemed impossible, but you tried your best anyway, and you did it?

Two years ago, I (Sheila) learned to ski. I have never been good at any sport. I have weak ankles, so I never learned to skate, and I am terrified of speed and heights. Besides that, skiing is expensive and we never could afford it. So, even though we live in Vail, which is regarded (at least by the locals) as the best ski resort in the world, Denny and I never learned to ski. John learned when he was four, thanks to friends who taught him for free.

Three years ago, John pleaded with us to learn and, like most parents, we'll do just about anything for our child. Once we let it be known that we wanted to learn to ski, it seemed the whole universe complied. Near-strangers donated equipment to us. Friends gave us free lessons (including one who is a world-class skier and flew in for a week to help us). And, that season Vail began offering a huge discount on season ski passes.

When I started, I couldn't get the skis on and I couldn't get them off. I didn't know how to get on the ski lift, so I asked the operators to slow it down, which annoyed everyone else. Then I fell getting off, so they had to stop it and come help me. I was so scared on the slightest hill that the first day I lurched backward and pulled a muscle in my leg. But I couldn't give up because I had promised John. And I learned to ski. I never knew it, and no one was more surprised than I, but I had skiing in me. If I can ski, you can do anything. Following is a process to help you get in touch with that.

## Healing Process: Impossible Dreams

1. Close your eyes, put your feet flat on the floor, and breathe deeply. Put your hand on your heart and breathe into it the love that permeates the entire universe, the love that fills the stars and the dirt and everything in between. Breathe out any fear, constriction or tension.
2. Recall a time when you did something that surprised you (and maybe everyone else, too), something you never thought you could do. Go back in your imagination to that moment and recall how you felt—perhaps wonder, amazement, delight in yourself—and let those feelings grow within you.
3. Imagine how you would change your world if you had all the resources you needed and knew you would succeed. What dream of yours would you make come true? What would you do? What would you try? How would you go about it? Who would you ask to join you?

   Run it in your mind like one of those inspirational videos. Experience it with all your senses as vividly as possible and enjoy it as much as you can.
4. Ask yourself, what first step could you take in the direction of making this dream come true?
5. When you are ready, gradually come back and open your eyes.

## Chapter 11

# WHAT ABOUT THE CHOCOLATE? HEALING THE FUTURE BY MEETING OUR NEEDS IN THE PRESENT

Several years ago we gave a retreat in Buenos Aires to two thousand people. To introduce a session on healing relationships with the deceased, Sheila said, “Many of you lost loved ones during the dictatorship. Thirty thousand people disappeared and were never seen again.” From one side of the room a voice yelled, “It was sixty thousand!” From the other side someone else yelled, “That’s all propaganda from Amnesty International! Very few people disappeared.” (We found out later that a group of generals’ wives were sitting there.) Soon people on both sides were screaming at each other, as if the conflict that had caused so much suffering in Argentina had broken out all over again.

We felt panic because the charged environment seemed so far removed from the caring one we were trying to create. Sheila said, “Everyone suffered during those years and people on both sides lost loved ones. We want to pray for healing of the grief you all share.” The screaming stopped and the room once again felt safe and caring.

Why was Sheila’s statement so effective? Despite her feeling of panic, she managed to verbalize the common need underneath the vastly different political positions in the room. Every human being has the same basic needs, in this case the need to grieve. Needs transcend ideological differences and give us a common language of compassion.

## Our Need to Get in Touch with Needs

As we read back over the manuscript for this book, we realize that all of the healing processes encourage the reader to get in touch with needs. As we look back even further, to all the other books we have written and all the retreats we have given, we see that the common theme throughout has been encouraging our audience to identify needs.

Sometimes this has gotten us in trouble, as when our first book (Denny and Matt's, written before Sheila joined us) encouraged readers to befriend their emotional needs in the process of forgiveness. That book, *Healing of Memories*,[1] was withdrawn from sale at some Christian conferences because the leaders believed we should ignore our own needs and forgive immediately. They told us that to do otherwise was "wallowing in emotion."

However, most of the problems confronting our world, some of which we have discussed in this book, are the result of being separated from our needs. In the example of the auditorium in Buenos Aires, two thousand people were fighting about whose perspective on the political struggle in Argentina was right. The result was a screaming match. In fact, both sides had something much more fundamental in common: the need to grieve the loss of loved ones.

The way out of those things that separate us from our light, such as competition, punishment and rewards, trances induced by the domination system and other issues discussed in this book, is to get in touch with our needs. This is true because needs are the life energy and the motivation behind every action. When we are in touch with our needs, we are in touch with our essential selves…with our light.

The hurts we experience in life are moments when our basic needs (for love, security, connection, respect, etc.) were not met. The auditorium in Buenos Aires was full of hurting people whose need to grieve had been largely unacknowledged. Healing became possible when this need was named and when everyone on both sides was given an opportunity to meet it by entering into a process of grieving. Moreover, once the group recognized a common need that was greater than their political differences, they were able to feel compassion for one another and recognize their common humanity. Hurts cannot cripple or divide us if we recognize our underlying needs, effectively communicate them and find ways to meet them.

## Nonviolent Communication

Although we have always recognized the importance of needs, the most useful tool we have found in recent years for discovering, communicating and meeting them is the process of Nonviolent Communication (or NVC), as developed by Marshall Rosenberg. This process is also known as "compassionate communication."[2]

Like the competitive way of playing musical chairs, our culture tends to assume that another's needs can be met only at the expense of our own. NVC is based upon a different assumption that we share, which is that we do not need to choose between meeting our needs and those of another. Everyone's needs can be met. We feel happiest when our own needs are met, and one of our most fundamental needs is to contribute to the well-being of others. We see this in the story of the vineyard workers who arrived late and received the same pay because the owner knew they needed it, or in John's delight in giving a large tip to the taco stand workers.

When we are in a crisis situation, as in the Buenos Aires auditorium, or in a conflict with a significant person, it can be difficult to believe solutions that meet everyone's needs are possible. However, the NVC process has been used successfully in interpersonal situations ranging from intimate relationships in families to opposing factions in war-torn countries, as well as in prisons, schools, corporations, government institutions and the like. Just as we changed the win/lose rules of the domination system in musical chairs and Jesus did the same with the Lord's Prayer, NVC changes the rules of communication so that everyone wins. Instead of communicating with judgments, guilt, shame, blame, threats of punishment, demands and such (all of which are based on domination and keep us in a trance), NVC creates a way of living and communicating through compassionate giving and receiving. In an environment of compassion, everyone's needs can be met.

We don't have to deal with two thousand screaming retreatants every day, but like most people we do have daily experiences of struggling to communicate with one another in the midst of seemingly conflicting needs. For example, I (Denny) often have to drive John someplace when I am running late. Following is a typical conversation:

Dennis: "John, we have to go right away. You'll be late for your piano lesson."

John: "Papa, it's only 3:00. We have plenty of time."

Dennis: "John, the last time we left at 3:00 we were ten minutes late. We have to go right now."

Usually such conversations end with John rolling his eyes and yet another round of him explaining why there is plenty of time.

In a situation like the conversation above, I have to ask myself the same question we often hear from parents when we speak about the uselessness of rewards and punishments: "If I can't punish and I can't reward, what can I do instead?" In the world of punishment and rewards, I could threaten, "I'm going to take your toys away for a week if you don't come right now." Or, I could promise, "If you come now, I'll buy you an ice cream after your piano lesson." The alternative is for John and me to meet each other's needs. We often use the four steps of the NVC process to help us do this.[a]

## Four Steps: Observation, Feelings, Needs, and Requests

Using my conversation with John as an example, I might speak to him using the four steps of NVC as follows:

Observation: John, I notice that it is 3:00 and you don't have your jacket on.

Feeling: I feel afraid because I'll have to drive too fast in order to get there on time.

Need: I want to leave now because I need safety for myself and for you.

Request: Would you be willing to get your jacket on and leave right away?

### STEP 1: OBSERVATION

The first step in NVC, or compassionate communication, is to share what I observe. This means I share the stimulus for my reaction by describing concretely what I notice with my senses. An observation is like a video camera, in that it records what is seen, heard, etcetera, that is affecting my well-being, without any evaluations or judgments. Thus, "John, I notice that it is 3:00 and you do not have your jacket on" is an observation. However, "I notice

[a]John now uses the NVC steps himself, but we began using this process before he had learned them. The NVC steps can be used effectively when only one person in the conversation is familiar with them.

For a parenting guide that avoids punishment and rewards, consistent with the principles of NVC, see Alfie Kohn, *Unconditional Parenting: Moving from Rewards and Punishment to Love and Reason* (New York: Atria, 2006), and his DVD program by the same title, available from www.unconditionalparenting.com (accessed February 10, 2011).

that you don't care about being on time," or, "I notice that you don't ever take the initiative to get ready on your own," are judgments and evaluations. They are counterproductive because they promote defensiveness and arguments, and diminish the possibility that John will be receptive to hearing my feelings and needs.

## STEP 2: FEELINGS

The second step of compassionate communication is sharing what I feel. When I say to John, "I feel afraid because I'll have to drive too fast," I move into the realm of feelings. These are emotional states or physical sensations resulting from our needs being met or not being met. Often after stating a feeling, such as, "I feel afraid," it helps to say "because I…" as I did with John: "…because I will have to drive too fast in order to get there on time." Using "because I" statements demonstrates that I am taking responsibility for whatever gives rise to my feelings. Since feelings focus on our inner experience, if I take responsibility for my feeling, I reveal myself in a way that enhances the possibility of making a heart connection with John.

Sometimes I mistakenly skip expressing the feeling, and use the words "I feel" to express, not a feeling, but a thought. If I were to say to John, "I feel that because you are late, I will not be able to drive carefully," or "I feel that you do not care about being on time," such statements are actually thoughts. A clue is that I could substitute the words "I think" for the words "I feel." Such thoughts contain judgments and evaluations. Because they place responsibility for my "feelings" on the actions of the other person, they can be heard as shaming or blaming. They are interpretations of what I think a person is doing, and they keep me from being vulnerable about what I am feeling.

Instead of saying that I feel abandoned (criticized, judged, betrayed, annoyed, misunderstood), which are assumptions about what the other person is doing to me, I can ask myself, "What am

I feeling when I think someone is abandoning me?" Perhaps the answer would be, "I feel alone," or "I feel sad." When I express such feelings as "aloneness" or "sadness," I make a heart connection with another and enhance the possibility of a response that will meet both of our needs. (See the appendix for a list of feelings.)

## STEP 3: NEEDS

The third step of compassionate communication is to share needs. Feelings reveal and lead to needs, since I experience distinct feelings when my needs are met (happy, alive, free, hopeful, trusting, etc.) and distinct feelings when my needs are not met (anxious, sad, edgy, resentful, uptight, etc.). Thus, after expressing what I feel, it is helpful to say, "...because I need...," as I did with John when I said, "...because I need safety." In this way I take responsibility for the needs behind my feelings.

Needs are the energy and the motivators behind the hundreds of actions that we do each day. Needs are universal. When I say to John, "I need safety," I am expressing a value, desire or necessity that all human beings share. A need such as safety (play, honesty, harmony, empathy, nourishment, shelter, etc.) is shared by everyone, although perhaps to varying degrees at different times.

Needs do not involve another person doing a specific action for me. For example, "I need connection" expresses a need, whereas, "I need for you to give me a hug" is a strategy for meeting my need. (Everyone needs connection, but not everyone needs a hug from you.) Needs free us from being attached to a specific request or strategy. By exploring the needs or various energies that motivate every action, we expand our capacity to dream so that once we move on to the final component of requesting that a person do a specific action for us, we will have many more possibilities for getting our needs met. (See the appendix for a list of the basic human needs we all share.)

## STEP 4: REQUEST

The fourth component of compassionate communication is a request. Requests are doable actions or strategies that would help me, and hopefully the other person, to each meet our needs. When I say to John, "Would you be willing to put on your jacket and get in the car right now?" I am asking for a specific, doable action that hopefully would meet both of our needs for safety. A request usually begins with, "Would you be willing…," since we are not demanding or insisting.

A request is doable when it involves a concrete *action*, such as, "Would you be willing to get in the car right now?" rather than how I want the other to *be*, as in, "Would you be willing to be on time (respectful, responsible, trustful, understanding, loving, an attentive listener, etc.)?" For example, instead of saying, "Would you be willing to listen to me?" I might ask, "Would you be willing to repeat back what you heard me say?"

We increase the likelihood of our request being met when we state it positively, as in, "Would you be willing to wait until I finish before you respond?" rather than negatively, as in, "Would you be willing to not interrupt me?" A request clearly expresses what concrete action I would like taken so that my and the other person's needs can be met.[b]

## HEALING PROCESS: FEELINGS AND NEEDS

(You may wish to refer to the lists of feelings and needs in the appendix.)

[b]There are many aspects of compassionate communication that go beyond the scope of this book. For example, what if I make a request and the other person says "No"? In John's case, he might refuse to leave immediately because he was afraid his need for play would not be met. Then we might continue using the four steps until we found a way to meet both his needs and mine. Or, I might find myself in a situation where the aprotective use of force" was required. See endnote 2 for resources on NVC by Marshall Rosenberg and his colleagues.

1. Think of a situation in which your needs were met. What specific needs were met? What were the feelings behind those needs?
2. Think of a situation in which your needs were not met. What specific needs were not met? What were the feelings behind those needs?

## What About the Chocolate?

The day we found the bag of chocolate hidden in John's closet was when he taught us about the importance of empathically hearing the needs behind every action. As mentioned in chapter 4, my (Denny's) first thought was some form of punishment, as I reverted to how my own parents would likely have handled such a situation when I was a child. What John had done seemed similar to when I reached for the box of chocolates in the cupboard and broke my mother's favorite cup. Both John and I were doing something we were not supposed to do. John feared what Sheila and I would say. I feared what my mother would say. John hid the evidence in the closet. I hid the evidence in the wastebasket by putting a large milk carton on top.

Before I would be able to compassionately communicate with John, I needed to give compassion to the frantic child I once was. As I listened for the needs behind my behavior, the ones that stood out were the needs to explore, to test boundaries and to celebrate. The one I still had was the need to celebrate. I promised to take myself out to lunch that day at my favorite Chinese restaurant.

Compassionate communication is, first, a way of living empathically with ourselves. Once we have received empathy, or once we have had our own feelings and needs heard, it is easier to give that same empathy to the person with whom we have a conflict. The four steps are tools for giving away the empathy that we have received.

After I had empathically cared for myself, I was ready to meet with Sheila and then care for John. Sheila and I first talked about our feelings of disappointment, our need for honesty and our need to keep John safe by providing healthy food for him. When we had listened empathically to one another, we felt ready to ask John to join us on the couch. After we got connected with him, the conversation went as follows:

Sheila: "John, we found this bag of chocolates in your closet. Can you tell us what happened?"

John: "When I put the chocolate in the closet, I felt afraid that if I asked you for some chocolate you'd say 'No.' I need more sweets than what you give me. I want you to let me decide how much chocolate I'm going to eat."

Sheila: "Are you saying you need more control over when you can eat sweet foods?"

John: "Yes, I want to choose when I can have chocolate."

Sheila: "How about if we give you a bag of organic chocolate chips? You can choose where to put them in the refrigerator. They're yours to eat as you wish, but not all at once. Let's say they should last two weeks. Then we'll get you more. The only other condition is that we want you to be able to fall asleep at night, so no chocolate chips after 6:00 p.m. How does that sound?"

John immediately agreed. Three months later, when we were cleaning out the refrigerator, we found the bag of chocolate chips still almost totally full. John had been clearly telling us that his action of hiding the chocolates had more to do with a need for autonomy than a desire for chocolate.

In this story, we didn't use the exact language of NVC that we just shared with you. What matters is that we were able to relate to John in the spirit of compassionate listening.[3] Perhaps, if John had spoken clear NVC, he might have sounded something like this:

Observation: The last three times I asked you if I could have something sweet, you said, "No."

Feeling: I feel afraid.

Need: Because I need to make choices.

Request: Would you be willing to allow me to make choices around how much candy I eat?

## Did We Get It Right?

We would only know if we "got it right" if everyone's needs were met. If John had consumed the entire package of chocolate chips the first day or if we discovered him hiding other things from us, then we would have had to explore what other needs of his were still not being met.

Compassionate communication is a way of holding another's reality and trying to care for it as best we can. For example, after our conversation with John, we began asking ourselves what other, if any, unexpressed needs might have caused him to hide chocolate in the closet. Were there too many restrictions in our home, and did he need more freedom to explore? Were there not enough restrictions in our home, and was he testing boundaries because he needed the security that clear boundaries provide? Was his metabolism too low so that he needed more high-energy foods? Did he need to celebrate more?

In subsequent conversations with John, we discovered that he needed more high-energy foods and more ways of celebrating. One of his requests was that he be able to make himself banana drinks whenever he wanted. Since then, we've worn out three blenders…

## Healing Process: The Four Steps of Compassionate Communication

(You may wish to refer to the lists of feelings and needs in the appendix.)

1. Think of a person who is difficult for you. Write down an observable behavior that you would like that person to change. (When I see, hear, etc.…)
2. Write down the feeling that observation activates in you. (I feel…)
3. Write down the unmet need behind your feeling. (…because I need…)
4. Write down a request or a concrete action that you would like the other person to do that would help meet your need. (Would you be willing…?)
5. Ask yourself if these four steps have given you any ideas about how you might relate to this person in the future.

## An Infinite Succession of Presents

This book is about healing the future, which can seem quite remote and full of daunting problems. How can we possibly have any significant effect upon it? Howard Zinn reminds us that "The future is an infinite succession of presents." In other words, we create the future by how we live in the present. If we live each day in the realm of cooperative musical chairs, where everyone wins and each person's needs are met, we are already healing the future. We are participating in a new kind of consciousness based upon our essential oneness.

We are all one because we all have the same basic needs. In this chapter, we have introduced compassionate communication, which is a way of communicating about our needs. The next chapter is about a daily process that we have used for many years to help us get in touch with those needs and do more of whatever helps us meet them.

Chapter 12

# MEETING OUR NEEDS EVERY DAY: SLEEPING WITH BREAD

> During the bombing raids of World War II, thousands of children were orphaned and left to starve. The fortunate ones were rescued and placed in refugee camps where they received food and good care. But many of these children who had lost so much could not sleep at night. They feared waking up to find themselves once again homeless and without food. Nothing seemed to reassure them. Finally, someone hit upon the idea of giving each child a piece of bread to hold at bedtime. Holding their bread, these children were finally able to sleep in peace. All through the night the bread reminded them, "Today I ate and I will eat again tomorrow."[1]

At the end of every evening, we turn off all the lights in the house and take time to remind ourselves that "Today I ate and I will eat again tomorrow." We begin by lighting an oil lamp. After taking a moment to get in touch with the light within us and within everything around us, we sit quietly while we ask ourselves two questions:

For what moment today am I most grateful?

For what moment today am I least grateful?

If the three of us are together, we share with each other our responses to those two questions. Since he was two years old, we

(Denny and Sheila) have done this process with John every evening before he falls asleep. It can also be done alone.

Our nightly ritual of examining our day is an adaptation of what St. Ignatius called the *examen*, and the two questions put us in touch with what he meant by *consolation* and *desolation*. Ignatius expected that by attending to consolation and desolation, we would become aware of the movement of the spirit within us.[a]

## We Experience Consolation and Desolation in Many Ways

We understand consolation as anything that helps us give and receive love. Desolation is whatever blocks our capacity to give and receive love. However, we might describe these two interior states in many other ways.

For example, we might begin at the physiological level. In chapter 2, we summarized the HeartMath research on the effects of holding a positive memory (a moment of consolation) briefly in our hearts. Our heart rate becomes coherent, and this entrains all the other systems of the body, resulting in an overall feeling of peace and well-being. This is how consolation feels in the body. Desolation, then, would be the state we're in when our heart rate is incoherent, with all the attendant feelings of dis-ease.

At the emotional level, we might speak of consolation as the experience of having our feelings heard and our needs met, consistent with the material in the previous chapter on nonviolent communication. Desolation, then, would be those moments when our feelings were not heard and our needs were not met.

[a]Our book for adults on the examen is *Sleeping with Bread: Holding What Gives You Life* (New York/Mahwah, NJ: Paulist Press, 1995). The children's version is *Making Heart-Bread* (New York/Mahwah, NJ: Paulist Press, 2006), which includes a section for parents and other caregivers on how to support children in reflecting daily on their consolation and desolation.

At another level—perhaps we'd call it the level of deeper meaning or the spiritual/soul level—we might say that consolation is when we remember our light and are in alignment with the "evolutionary impulse"[2] that expresses itself through us and through every other aspect of the universe. Often Sheila and I (Denny) do the examen outside in our hammock beneath the star-lit sky. We usually snuggle together inside a double sleeping bag, so that we can do the examen outside even in cold weather.

When I look up at the night sky, I feel awe as I wonder how I got from being stardust to arriving in the hammock. I realize that the spirit that has moved within everything in the entire cosmos for 13.7 billion years—from the Great Radiance, to the formation of stars, to their explosion into stardust, to the formation of my body that lies in the hammock as I consciously reflect upon my experience of love and connection—is the same cosmic spirit that has moved inside of me all day. Thus, the movements within open me to 13.7 billion years of wisdom. This new understanding allows me to own that I am not contained in my body. Rather, my spirit extends through space and time and thus allows me to own myself as being as vast and as wise as the cosmos itself.

My moments of consolation during the day are those times when I have been most in touch with the evolutionary impulse, the movement of the spirit encouraging me (and the entire universe) toward the next step in my evolution. Desolation, for me, marks those times when I have been most out of touch with how the spirit has been encouraging me. The question, then, is how can I listen to and learn from the movements of consolation and desolation within me?

## Returning to Moments of Consolation

In the Spiritual Exercises, St. Ignatius advises us to keep returning to moments of consolation, especially when we are experiencing desolation. This suggestion seems to tap into an ancient wisdom that is practiced by many peoples, such as the Babemba tribe of South Africa. In that tribe,

> When a person acts irresponsibly or unjustly, he is placed in the center of the village, alone and unfettered. All work ceases, and every man, woman and child in the village gathers in a large circle around the accused individual. Then each person in the tribe speaks to the accused, one at a time each recalling the good things the person in the center of the circle has done in his lifetime. Every incident, every experience that can be recalled with any detail and accuracy, is recounted. All his positive attributes, good deeds, strengths, and kindnesses are recited carefully and at length. This tribal ceremony often lasts for several days. At the end, the tribal circle is broken, a joyous celebration takes place, and the person is symbolically and literally welcomed back into the tribe.[3]

This story reminds us of the circle of people that gathered around John when we (Denny and Sheila) celebrated his baptism. We began by reading the account of Jesus' baptism, in which Jesus hears a voice from heaven saying, "You are my Son, the Beloved; with you I am well pleased" (Mark 1:11). Then we asked our eighty guests to each get in touch with what they were most grateful for about John. How was John a beloved son who delighted them? One after another, they came forward and blessed whatever gift they appreciated most in John. One person, noticing John's ability to maintain eye contact for long periods of time, blessed his gift of intimate relationship. Others blessed his gifts of joy, focused awareness, sense of humor and so forth. The community's blessing of these gifts was a commitment to gratefully remember and encourage John's gifts throughout his life.

Returning to moments of gratitude, as the Babemba do when one of their members misbehaves, is fundamental to emotional healing. We return in our hearts to John's baptism whenever he engages in some typical childish misbehavior. On such occasions, we put our arms around him and begin by encouraging him to put his hand on his heart and breathe deeply. Then we share with him our memories of his goodness, such as the many times when he has gone out of his way to do something kind for another person or come to tell us immediately that he has broken something.

As we share these memories, John seems to come back to himself, as if reconnecting with his own goodness. Only then do we encourage him to reflect on his behavior and how he can make amends for any damage done. John recovers from minor childhood misbehavior by focusing on positive images of himself, which allows him to gratefully remember who he is and who he wants to become.[b]

John seems to have understood from a very early age the principle of returning to consolation during moments of desolation. For example, by the time he was only a few months old, our family had discovered "The Coughing Game." Whenever any one of us coughed, the other two would cough as well and then we'd all laugh. The point of the game seemed to be, "We belong together."

When John was eight months old, we were on an airplane destined for Mexico. We'd been up a lot with him the night before

[b]This process of encouraging the child to remember who he or she is can be done at any time. We do this with John on birthdays, on New Year's Eve and at other special moments. See our book for children, *What Is My Song?* (New York/Mahwah, NJ: Paulist Press, 2004), which includes a section for parents and other caregivers who want to support children in remembering their unique song.

and then had to leave early for the airport. We were exhausted and not looking forward to several hours on a plane with a squirmy baby. Then, as we waited on the runway, the pilot announced that our flight was delayed because of mechanical problems, and we would need to stay in our seats. John started fussing and Denny, who hadn't an ounce of energy or patience left, snapped at him, "John!!"

Neither we nor anyone else had ever spoken sharply to John before. His eyes got really big and he stared at his father, stared at his mother and then…he coughed. We got it right away. Denny coughed in return and so did Sheila. Then we all laughed. When we were in desolation, our eight-month-old baby had led the way and reminded us to return to the consolation of knowing that we belong together.

## Positive Thoughts Don't Make Everything OK

Returning to moments of consolation for which we are grateful, like any potent medicine, can be abused. For example, gratitude is often associated with positive thinking, and sometimes seems to be used as a way to deny or manipulate the painful aspects of life. Many self-help books, tapes, courses, motivational speakers and media stars encourage us to count our blessings, think positively and imagine things as we want them to be, on the theory that what you see is what you get. According to this way of thinking, our perception of reality makes it so. Since anything negative is only an illusion, it will cease to exist if we don't pay attention to it.

There is some validity to such ideas, given the power of energy signals such as positive intention. However, this works only if we're telling the truth about ourselves. It doesn't work if we are using positive thoughts in an attempt to lie about or otherwise override and control negative feelings. The results can be frustrating (and can also encourage the tendency to blame people who are poor, sick, etc., for their problems).[4]

Retreatants have sometimes asked us, "I heard that if I wrote down a list of five affirmations about myself, taped my list to the mirror and read it every day, I would start to believe those things and feel good about myself. Why do I still feel so bad?" You still feel so bad because feelings are prior to and more influential than thoughts. Painful feelings don't go away because we use positive thinking as a pair of rose-colored glasses.[c]

We (Denny and Matt) saw in our own family how much harm this can do. When our brother died at the age of two, our parish priest told our mother, "Don't be sad. Be grateful because now you have a saint in heaven." She obeyed and swallowed her grief, as well as her fear that tragedy might befall another of her children. Thus, she never fully grieved the loss of her son and thereby lost a part of

---

[c]Recent research demonstrates that the common assumption that thoughts are prior to and more influential than feelings is incorrect:

> The basic theoretical framework is that if emotions always follow thought, then by changing one's thoughts, one can gain control over the emotions. However, in the last decade, research in the neurosciences has made it quite clear that emotional processes operate at a much higher speed than thoughts, and frequently bypass the mind's linear reasoning process entirely. In other words, not all emotions follow thoughts: many (and in fact most in certain contexts) occur independently of the cognitive systems and can significantly bias or color the cognitive process and its output or decision.
>
> This is why strategies that encourage "positive thinking" without also engaging positive feelings may frequently provide only temporary, if any, relief from emotional distress.

R. McCraty and D. Tomasino, "Coherence Building Techniques and Heart Rhythm Coherence Feedback: New Tools for Stress Reduction, Disease Prevention and Rehabilitation," in E. Molinari, A. Compare and G. Parati, eds., *Clinical Psychology and Heart Disease* (New York: Springer, 2006), 490–91.

Also, unconscious beliefs are much more powerful than conscious ones and override positive thinking: According to Bruce Lipton, "...the subconscious mind is millions of times more powerful than the conscious mind....You can repeat the positive affirmation that you are lovable over and over or that your cancer tumor will shrink. But if, as a child, you heard over and over that you are worthless and sickly, those messages programmed in your subconscious mind will undermine your best conscious efforts to change your life." Dr. Lipton believes that, because unconscious messages are embedded in our energetic system, they are best dealt with through energetic methods. Bruce Lipton, *The Biology of Belief* (New York: Hay House, 2008), 97–98, 173–75.

herself. For the rest of her life, our mother had a limited range of emotions, the most prevalent of which was fear. She especially feared painful feelings. Her typical response to other people who expressed painful feelings in her presence was to discount their feelings and tell them to be grateful...as the priest had told her.

Our mother taught us that the deepest fear most of us struggle with is fear of negative feelings. It's not our feelings themselves that keep us stuck but rather fear of our feelings that prevents us from gratefully welcoming them so that we can hear their story.[5] If our mother could have been lovingly present to her grief and fear, her feelings would have shifted naturally. We doubt she would still have been emotionally paralyzed fifty years later.

Perhaps in part because we have seen the suffering that misused positive thinking can cause, our position is quite different from the rose-colored glasses approach. Also, a formative influence in our lives is Ignatian spirituality, which is based upon finding the movement of the spirit in all things, including all emotions. We assume that all of life, even our most painful moments, has something to offer us when we care for ourselves exactly as we are, without trying to change or fix how we feel, and are gratefully open to the gifts that painful experiences can bring us.

Moreover, using positive thoughts to control negative feelings doesn't work because in so doing we violate the dynamic and inherently meaningful nature of negative emotions. If we follow the natural movement of negative emotions, such as anger and fear, and embrace them with the same loving, caring presence with which we embrace our friends, they will transform themselves from within. Like our friends, every negative feeling—whether momentary annoyance or profound terror—has a story to tell. Once the story of any emotion is heard, it resolves itself naturally, enriching and deepening our inner life in the process.[6] Negative feelings remain stuck only when we try to override or repress them rather than hearing their story and responding to the needs they reveal.

## Listening to Desolation: Every Feeling Has a Story to Tell

How can we hear the story of our feelings, especially the ones that seem stuck or overwhelming? Perhaps the care most of us feel for children can help us. When John was younger, if he felt frightened, sad, tired or frustrated, he would say, "Mama, hold me!" I (Sheila) always picked him up as quickly as possible and held him. What was he really asking for? I am sure the physical comfort of being in my arms was part of it. But I think he was asking for something more, as well. He was asking me to hold in my heart, or contain for him, aspects of his reality that would be overwhelming for him if he were alone. John still needs this from Denny and me, although now that he's bigger than us, we put our arms around him rather than picking him up.

John's need to be held has many layers, some of which I can guess because I am with him so closely. When he was little and woke up in the night crying, "Hold me," I carried in my heart not only his fear of being alone in the dark but also when he fell and skinned his knee that morning, the frightening image of war that he saw on the front page of a newspaper as we walked through town, and other painful moments from the day. John doesn't wake up in the night anymore, but when he is upset I still verbalize for him what I think his feelings might be trying to say, and I know I have guessed correctly when his breathing deepens and his body relaxes. Mostly, I carry the whole story in my heart as I hug him and assure him that Papa and I are there and he is safe.

What if Denny or I were not there when John cried, "Hold me!"? What if we agreed with the 44 percent of American parents who believe they'll spoil a baby if they pick him up when he cries?[7] As an adult, John might still be carrying those same overwhelming feelings. Perhaps he would withdraw from relationships in fear that no one could be trusted. Perhaps he would act out in the form of a relationship addiction, asking one random person after another to "Hold me!"

Or, what if we did go to John when he cried and said, "There is nothing to be afraid of. Go back to sleep"? Perhaps, in later life, he would tell himself to think positively and lose a vital connection to his interior life (as Agnes May did), rather than developing the capacity to be grateful for all his feelings. Our hope is that the way we hold John is helping him develop a lifelong habit of giving his feelings a loving, caring presence so they can tell him their story.[8]

## Burger King Next Exit

I (Matt) try to hold all my feelings as Sheila holds John. For example, one day I was driving from Minneapolis to Milwaukee with my mother, who was in the early stages of Alzheimer's disease. As we traveled, she read the highway signs aloud to me. She had been a reading teacher, and perhaps this made her feel useful. Perhaps it reminded her of when her mind was whole and she taught many children to read, including me. She read each sign in a loud voice: "Burger King 3 Miles…Truckers Welcome…Burger King This Exit…Playground for Kids…Burger King, Hungry for a Whopper?" I suggested she say her rosary. "Holy Mary, Mother of God, pray for us…Burger King Next Exit…Have It Your Way…now and at the hour of our death. Amen."

Desperately, I tried to get my mother to focus on the beautiful fall trees. I told her I could read the signs and didn't need any help. After about twenty seconds of golden silence, she would forget what I had just said and start again: "Pepsi Cola, The Pause That Refreshes." I turned on the radio and then a tape, but she gave no refreshing pause. Full of anger at my mother, my hands gripped the steering wheel and I wished I could control her as well as I could control the car. I renewed my efforts to silence her. "Rest Stop Next Exit," she said.

I panicked because I conservatively estimated there were ten signs per mile. That meant she would read me 3,410 signs by the time we got to Milwaukee. I pulled into the rest stop so I could get a few minutes of quiet. I got out of the car, put my hand on my heart and tried to care for my feelings, as I would have cared for a hurt child. Beneath my anger I felt fear that by the time I arrived in Milwaukee I would be totally frazzled and unable to focus on the retreat I was scheduled to give.

As I let myself be with these feelings rather than pushing them away, the road ahead of me became the future rather than the way to Milwaukee. I saw my mother traveling that road and I knew that soon she would be too confused to recognize signs or recognize me. I stayed with my anxiety and realized my deepest fear was that some day maybe I, too, would spend months or years on a similar journey. Would I end up lost in confusion and unable to communicate?

As I embraced this fear, my feelings shifted. I became aware of how much I loved my mother, no matter how confused she was. I knew that I would look back on this trip as a special moment my mother and I had shared while she could still read. She was clinging to it as the only thing still normal in her advancing senility.

I got back into the car. For the rest of the trip, her reading was like background music, teaching me her way of letting go of what she could no longer do and yet fully entering into what she still could do. She was giving me a short course on how to survive the journey I feared most—her journey into senility if ever it were mine. With each breath I gratefully let my love for her grow within me, just the way she was.

I knew, too, how the spirit would still be within me and how others would still love me if one day I had to go on a journey like my mother's. My fear of disconnection from love was beginning to heal, as well, as I smiled and gratefully enjoyed each sign she could still read. We were both loved. That was the last time we traveled together. A year later she couldn't read or hardly speak a sentence. That trip is now one of my fondest memories.

During her final years, my mother was the most difficult person in my life. She was so difficult because she reflected back to me what I still to some extent feared most in myself. My feelings toward my mother were often my desolation during that time. As I learned to embrace those feelings and listen to their story, I was able to be with my mother and with the parts of myself that I had projected onto her. In this way, listening to my desolation helped me heal my deepest fear.

## Healing Process for Desolation[d]

1. Sit comfortably with your eyes closed. Let your awareness move down into the center of your body and notice what you feel there.
2. Ask yourself, "What keeps me from feeling really good right now?" Perhaps it is some area of your life where you feel stuck, overwhelmed, out of control or powerless. Perhaps it is a painful feeling that keeps recurring, an old wound that you continually replay in your mind or something else in your life that you wish were different.
3. Ask yourself if you want to listen to this part of yourself right now. Is it ok to spend some time with it? If not, care for the feeling of not wanting to spend time with this right now.
4. If it is ok to spend some time with this area of your life, take a few moments to create a loving atmosphere where it will feel safe to speak to you. For example, how would you reach out to a wounded child?
5. Now let yourself down into how this whole thing feels inside of you. Where in your body do you especially experience it?

[d]It may be helpful to ask another person to lead you through these steps, which are our adaptation of a process known as "focusing." For guidance in leading another, see Edwin McMahon and Peter Campbell, *The Focusing Steps* (Kansas City: Sheed and Ward, 1991).

Perhaps you feel as if someone were hitting you on the head or pulling on your arm. Perhaps you feel a knot in your stomach, a lump in your throat, shaking in your legs, etcetera.

6. Care for this feeling and see if it wants to tell you about itself, perhaps through a word, an image or a symbol. Perhaps it wants to come to you as a little child. Perhaps it wants to tell you its name, its history (when and how it developed) and what it needs.
7. Whatever comes, reach out to care for it without trying to change it or fix it. Or, maybe just put your hand on that part of your body in a caring way.
8. Tell this part of you that you will come back at another time and listen to it some more.
9. Before concluding, notice how your body feels compared to when you began. Are you now carrying this issue differently in your body? Give thanks for whatever change has taken place.

## Field of Dreams: Listening to Desolation and Returning to Consolation

Several years ago, because of a painful family situation, my (Denny's) normally close relationship with my father was strained. My father was aging and I was afraid he would die without us being reconciled. What could I do? When I listened to the story behind my desolation (my feelings of disappointment and sadness) I felt a need for connection. Then an image came to me of how to meet that need: I would kidnap my father.

Since leaving home at seventeen, I had written to my parents at least twice every week. I decided to continue this despite the strain in my relationship with my father. Beginning in November of that year and for the following nine months, I ended every letter with the same warning: "Dad, on the sixth of August, I am coming to town to kidnap you."

On August sixth, I arrived in Minneapolis and asked my father if he was ready to be kidnapped. He replied that he wasn't going anywhere with me. He had discovered that on August ninth our family was planning a surprise eightieth birthday party for him. My father informed me that he needed three days to prepare for his surprise party.

My father was very stubborn, and so am I. We sat down to negotiate. He finally agreed that he would allow me to kidnap him if he could drive. Thus, we left our family home in Minneapolis and drove for nine hours through Minnesota and Iowa. I said, "Go right…go left…go straight," and my kidnapped father obediently followed every instruction.

My father grew up on a farm, and that day I learned more about corn than I ever wanted to know. Finally, we arrived at the farming community of Dyersville, Iowa. "We have arrived," I said. "Make a sharp turn to the right." Directly in front of us was an enormous cornfield. My puzzled father said, "What am I supposed to do now?" I replied, "I want you to go into the cornfield and listen for voices."

After hours of confinement in the car, my father happily jumped out and walked into the cornfield. After twenty minutes or so, he returned.

"Did you hear any voices?" I asked.

"No, was I supposed to?"

"Maybe it's because you're tired out from the trip. Let's go over there and play baseball."

Hesitantly, he agreed to play catch. As we were throwing the ball back and forth, he grumbled, "We could have done this at home in the backyard."

That evening I checked us into a local motel and went back out to pick up a movie that I had reserved months before. When

I returned to the motel, my father had fallen asleep. So ended his first day of kidnapping.

The next morning I played the movie, *Field of Dreams*. It tells the story of a broken relationship between a father and a son and how listening for voices in a cornfield and playing baseball reunites them. The film was produced in Dyersville and, unbeknownst to my father, on the previous day I had taken him to the same cornfield and baseball diamond. It wasn't long before he was watching intently and telling me, "That's the cornfield where you told me to listen for voices yesterday." (How anyone can distinguish one cornfield in Iowa from another is beyond me.)

When the movie was over, I shared with my father all of the dreams he had helped me to carry out. For example, beginning when I was eleven years old, Matt and I spent the first part of the summer in the library. We would read about faraway places like Quebec, New York City, Washington, DC, and Juarez, Mexico. Then at the end of the summer, Matt and I decided where we wanted to go. For two or three weeks I told my father, "Go right... go left...go straight." In this way, each year we went on five or six thousand miles of back roads with our parents.

That day in the motel in Dyersville, I shared with my father how those childhood trips had helped me feel at home in unknown places and with people from varied backgrounds. We have given retreats in over sixty countries, and I told him that every time I go to a new country, I am completing the childhood dream he gave me of being at home anywhere in the world.

My father was obviously moved. With tears in his eyes, he said, "Let's watch the movie again." When *Field of Dreams* ended for the second time, I shared with him even more dreams that he had given me. Then we hugged, kissed and cried. My father looked me in the eye and said, "This is probably the happiest day of my life."

From that moment until his death five years later, my father was quite different. Previously he had tended to tell me what I should think and feel. But on the way back to Minneapolis, he asked me about my dreams, and he spent the rest of his life helping me fulfill them. I changed, too. I had tended to be compliant in my relationship with my father. But that trip gave me confidence that I could share my dreams with him and complete them, even if they were different from his expectations of me.

Why did so much healing happen on that trip to the field of dreams? As we recalled our family trips during my childhood, our hearts were flooded with gratitude for the love we had felt for one another then, and the certainty that we would stick together no matter what. We were reminded of the core of our relationship, and our hope was renewed that we could be at least that close again. St. Ignatius would not have been surprised that so much healing happened, since I had followed his suggestions. I had listened to the story behind my desolation and its surprising answer: to kidnap my father. I had also followed Ignatius's suggestion that whenever we are stuck in desolation, we should return to moments of consolation. Those childhood trips were such moments, as we shared beauty and dreams with one another, and made friends with the strangers we met along the way.

One way to describe the healing my father and I experienced is to say that we remembered who we were by remembering shared moments of consolation. This helped us recover a way of being together that was healthy and life-giving. Returning to consolation not only heals hurts from the past but also opens us to the vastness of who we can be in the future. Researchers at the Institute of HeartMath describe the expansive effect on everyday life of returning to moments of consolation—what we might describe as living in a field of dreams:

> You feel a deep sense of peace and internal balance—you are at harmony with yourself, with others, and with your larger environment. You experience increased buoyancy

> and vitality. Your senses are enlivened—every aspect of your perceptual experience seems richer, more textured. Surprisingly, you feel invigorated even when you would usually have felt tired and drained. Things that usually would have irked you just don't "get to you" as much. Your body feels regenerated—your mind is clear. At least for a period of time, decisions become obvious as priorities clarify and inner conflict dissolves. Intuitive insight suddenly provides convenient solutions to problems that had previously consumed weeks of restless thought. Your creativity flows freely. You may experience a sense of greater connectedness with others and feelings of deep fulfillment.[9]

## A Closing Parenthesis

All our retreats are bounded by two processes, rather like an opening parenthesis at the beginning and a closing one at the end. The opening one is getting in touch with positive memories, as we discussed in chapter 2. The closing parenthesis, as we approach the end of this book, is the examen. We emphasize the importance of the examen to newly married couples, parents, members of communities and individuals...to anyone who wants to grow in intimacy with themselves and others. Educator John Taylor Gatto expresses well why we value the examen so much:

> To know yourself, you have to keep track of your random choices, figure out your patterns, and use this knowledge to dominate your own mind....If you avoid this, other minds will manipulate and control you lifelong.[10]

## Healing Process: The Examen

(You may wish to do this process with another person.)

1. Close your eyes. Breathe deeply and slowly. Let your attention move down into your heart and imagine that you are breathing in and out through your heart.
2. Ask yourself, "For what moment today am I most grateful?" Let yourself relive that moment in your imagination, as you continue to breathe deeply through your heart. Ask yourself what was so special about that experience.
3. Now ask yourself, "For what moment today am I least grateful?" Hold whatever comes, giving it a loving, caring presence as you listen to its story.
4. If you are with another person, take a few minutes to share as much as you wish of your responses to the two questions.

## Chapter 13

# COMING OUT FROM UNDER THE CLOUD

As we did the examen each day during the past few years, our desolation often had to do not so much with events in our own lives, but rather with our growing awareness that something is really wrong in our world. We (Denny and Sheila) remember walking together while we were in the midst of this, sharing our fear for John and the kind of society he would have to live in. One of us asked the other, "Do you remember what it was like when we used to take for granted that we would have a future?" We were referring to a time only a few years earlier, but so much had changed during those few years that everything seemed dim and uncertain, as if the whole universe had gone under a cloud.

As we came to terms with the reality of our world and addressed the personal wounding it activated within ourselves, we began to emerge from under the cloud. Although our realization of how very wrong some things are has continued to grow, our hope for the future has also grown as we've opened ourselves to a completely new kind of consciousness that is emerging within and around us. In this chapter, we want to share our journey of coming out from under some of the darker aspects of that cloud.

There are many issues that affect us all, such as escalating violence, global warming, environmental pollution, the coarsening of our culture and its effect on our children, or signs of an economic collapse that has already left many without jobs or retirement funds. In what follows, we will focus on a few of the issues that most affected us. You may have different information than ourselves and see the world in a different way. Although the focus of your concerns may be different from ours, we hope the process we will share will help you with whatever issues concern you most.

## Outer and Inner Worlds

Part of the difficulty of facing what's wrong in the outer world is that it often activates unresolved wounds in our inner world. For example, a colleague of ours, a prominent psychotherapist who supervises other therapists, told us the following story. At the beginning of the first Gulf War, in 1990, President George H. W. Bush announced on national television that we were about to begin military operations against Iraq. He emphasized the nobility of the war effort and implicitly defined patriotism as unquestioning support for it, so that anyone who disagreed felt pressured to keep quiet.

In the days that followed, psychotherapists in his area told our colleague that they had noticed a significant increase in the number of clients who reported memories of incest. He speculated that hearing a father figure (the president of the country) announce something they perceived as violent and bad and call it something good, reminded them of their own fathers doing the same to them and telling them to keep quiet.

The point of this story is not a political one. Some of our readers may believe that the first Gulf War was necessary. Others, especially those who are committed to nonviolence, may believe it was a terrible mistake. Our point is that, regardless of one's political position, world events affect our personal lives and can activate our unhealed wounds.

For example, many of my (Sheila's) Jewish ancestors were killed in Nazi-occupied Europe, in part through the complicity of their neighbors and through the "silence of good people," such as church officials. Although I was not yet born at that time, I carry a deep, ancestral knowing of the terror of genocide and a determination never to be one of those silent, good people. Yet, I don't know how to scream loud enough to stop my country's violence against others.

Our friend Tom wants to scream in a different way. Tom served in the army during World War II, when he was very young. He believes that he helped save the world from tyranny. He describes his years of military service as the best time of his life, because he felt a sense of belonging with his comrades and of purpose in defending his country. After the war Tom entered the priesthood, because he wanted to continue a life of service. For Tom, U.S. military leaders and the president are the strong fathers he never had. When Tom hears criticism of these people, he feels fear and outrage. He, too, wants to scream. His scream might sound something like this: "Don't take away what saved my life and gives it meaning!"

In the stories of the incest victims and of Sheila and Tom, societal events in the present activated personal wounds in the past. Because societal wounding and personal wounding are so mutually reinforcing, we will try to weave them together in what follows.

## Things Are Not as They Appear

Our journey begins with the 2004 election. We (Denny and Sheila) and John, who was seven at the time, worked very hard to elect a particular candidate. On the morning after election day, we learned he had lost. John was heartbroken and said, "It was all for nothing!" We were heartbroken, too, but we told John, "We did our best and that's always worth it."

We tried to turn the experience into a civics lesson, and explained to John that in a democratic society, sometimes more people want a different candidate than you do, and elections are determined by the majority. We wanted him to understand that the process of democratic elections is more important in the long run than who wins or loses, and we wanted him to trust that process. Then we found out that none of us could trust the process, when we learned of carefully researched evidence that the election was fraudulent. In fact, our candidate had most likely won by a significant margin. Nevertheless, his opponent took office.[1]

At that point, the media-induced trance we had been in cracked open. The world was not at all as it had appeared to be. Our experience of working with addicts and their families had taught us how crazy-making it is to live in a world where what we're told is the direct opposite of what is really going on. At some subconscious level, perhaps cellular or energetic, all of us know whether what we are told is true or not true. If we deny what we know and accept a definition of reality that contradicts it, we lose contact with ourselves and our power to act in the world. Perhaps this is why the Twelve-Step recovery movement emphasizes that we are as sick as our secrets.

Whether the secrets are familial or societal, we didn't want that kind of sickness for John or for ourselves. Nor did we want John, who was already reading the Declaration of Independence and the Constitution, to lose totally his trust that democracy can work. So, we decided to find out how a fraudulent election was possible.

I (Sheila) went with two computer experts to test the electronic voting machines at our county clerk's office. Although we had no reason to suspect our county clerk, it was evident to all of us how easily those machines could be manipulated at local levels as well as at the state level of collating vote totals from each county. We learned that many candidates are supported by powerful interests who encourage the manufacture and use of the machines, and that voting machines are only one aspect of a complex strategy to disenfranchise voters.[2] These powerful corporate interests benefit from electing officials who will cooperate with the cycle of war, addiction to fossil fuels, environmental pollution, the resulting illnesses from which drug companies profit, and the exploitation of poor people around the world.

One thing led to another, as it so often does when we open a new door. For example, we learned that we could have eliminated the use of fossil fuels at least as long ago as the 1950s and that information about safe alternatives has been suppressed.[3] And we learned that the basis of the Iraq War (and virtually all previous wars) was a lie.[4]

## Addicted to War

As of this writing, although our military has been withdrawn from Iraq, we still have private contractors there. The war in Iraq led to a war in Afghanistan that has now bled into Pakistan. How did we get into the Iraq war, which most of us now realize was a mistake? The simple answer is through lies, such as that Iraq had weapons of mass destruction, that Saddam Hussein had ties to Osama bin Laden and that our motive was to bring democracy to Iraq. Our government lied to us as a pretext for starting a preemptive, illegal war of aggression against Iraq that even prominent administration officials who supported the war, such as Alan Greenspan (former chairman of the Federal Reserve) and Paul Wolfowitz (former head of the World Bank), have acknowledged was really about oil.[5]

This pattern of behavior on America's part, of seeking opportunities for war, is not new. President Eisenhower tried to warn against it when he said on April 16, 1953,

> Every gun that is made, every warship launched, every rocket fired signifies, in the final sense, a theft from those who hunger and are not fed, those who are cold

> and are not clothed. The world in arms is not spending money alone. It is spending the sweat of its laborers, the genius of its scientists, the hopes of its children....This is not a way of life at all, in any true sense. Under the cloud of threatening war, it is humanity hanging from a cross of iron.[6]

In the four decades after President Eisenhower said this, America spent more than $15 trillion to build up its military might. That adds up to more than the cumulative monetary value of all human-made wealth up to that point. Thus, we spent more on the military during those four decades than the value of all the factories, machinery, roads, bridges, water and sewage systems, airports, railroads, power plants, office buildings, shopping centers, schools, hospitals, hotels, houses, etcetera, in the country put together.[7] In Lawrence Wittner's paraphrase of Martin Luther King, "A nation that spends more money on war than life is approaching spiritual death."[8]

Not only spiritual death but also economic collapse. The concern that currently seems to preoccupy Americans most is the economy and the high rate of unemployment. If one questions military spending, as we just did, a common response is that more jobs would be lost and the economy would be even worse. In fact, spending a billion dollars on the production of guided missiles would create nine thousand jobs. If we spent that same billion dollars on pollution control, sixteen thousand jobs would be created. If we spent it on local transit, twenty-one thousand jobs would be created. And, if we spent it on educational services, sixty-three thousand jobs would be created.[9] Instead of exacerbating our economic and jobs crisis, reducing military spending and using the money for peaceful, life-affirming purposes would alleviate it.

The money we have spent on war could have fed, housed and educated billions of poor people around the world, nearly half of whom earn less than two dollars per day.[10] This would give us real "security," since the vast majority of human beings want only to provide for their families and have no interest in violence or terrorism when their needs are met. Instead, we've behaved as addicts, spending all the family's money on alcohol or drugs instead of providing food for ourselves and our children.

Like most untreated addictions, our condition seems to be worsening, as serial war becomes the "American way of life":

> ...in the history of the United States war has never been considered the normal state of things. For two centuries, Americans were taught to think war itself an aberration, and "wars" in the plural could only have seemed doubly aberrant. Younger generations of Americans, however, are now being taught to expect no end of war—and no end of wars.[11]

## Early Wounds

Trying to take in all of this during a short period of time, as well as many other even more alarming issues that we have not even mentioned here, was traumatic. For about a year we had symptoms similar to posttraumatic stress disorder (PTSD), such as fear, confusion, disorientation, helplessness and despair. Moreover, if we accepted all this, what else might be true and where might it lead us...in other words, if we went down the rabbit hole, would we ever get back out?

All of this activated our own early wounds, just as George H. W. Bush's announcement of the first Gulf War seemed to activate the incest wounds of some members of his television audience. One form of being in a trance is to believe that abusive parents were really trying to love and care for us. If we were to face the abusive aspects of our government (which we want to believe will take care of us), those of us who came from unsafe families might have to face the abusive aspects of our own parents (who we want to believe did take care of us).

For example, I (Sheila) grew up in an unsafe environment. I was told to keep quiet about it. When I tried to talk about what I experienced, I was not believed, and I concluded that it was my fault. This aspect of my early life and its consequences for my inner world directly paralleled my later experience in the outer world described above, of discovering that aspects of that world are far more unsafe than I had realized and that people who tell the truth about such things are ridiculed and silenced. The combination of inner wounds and what I was learning about the outer world left me in a state of considerable anxiety and self-doubt for about a year.

I (Denny) grew up wanting peace at any price and trying as best I could to not rock the boat. This had many roots, including a strict, religious upbringing in which I was taught that authorities (beginning with the priest and by extension all authorities) knew the truth and would keep me safe, so I could just get on with my life. I didn't want to question authorities and I wanted someone else to take care of it for me. I had enough to do in my own life, and I didn't want to be bothered with more because I saw my time and my resources as scarce. As I learned that I really couldn't trust some of the sources of authority I had relied on, I was afraid I would be overwhelmed and never get my own life back.

I (Matt) grew up in the same family as Denny and share many of the same issues. In addition, I was conceived two months after Pearl Harbor, a supposedly surprise attack that left my family and the entire country in a state of emergency alert. This was the energetic environment in which I developed in the womb. My birth was extremely difficult and involved a desperate effort on my part to get out or die. Moreover, I was always the shortest kid and afraid of any violence, because I knew I couldn't defend myself. I want a safe world, and I didn't want to look at anything that might exacerbate my fear of being unprotected.

## What Helped Us?

It was during the time when we were learning about the issues in this chapter that we visited our friend Jim. As we mentioned in the introduction, he told us we looked more scared than he'd ever seen us. We told him all that we've written in this chapter (and more). As we reflected with Jim on our inner state, we realized we had symptoms reminiscent of PTSD. We also told him how difficult it was for us to write, even though we had published a new book almost every year in the past and felt a real urgency to offer something that would be healing for our audience in the midst of all the trouble in the world around us. It was then that Jim said, "Notice what helps you. That is what you have always written about, and that will be your next book." True to Jim's words, the chapters of this book are what helped us with the PTSD-like distress we felt about the state of our world and with the inner wounding those issues had activated in each of us. Every process we have included is one we did ourselves and that helped us recover.

Our starting point was the examen, introduced in chapter 12. As we reflected each evening on what had given us consolation and desolation that day, we found the next step in healing. For example, as we listened to our desolation, it told us what it needed.

When our desolation took the form of a sense of heaviness and darkness, we needed to recall our light and go back to positive memories of love (see chapters 1 and 2).

When we wondered if we were failures in some way because we were questioning consensual reality and feared we might even be punished for it, we needed to grow in freedom from competition, punishment and rewards (see chapters 3, 4, 5 and 6).

When we felt dazed by it all and, struggling to hold on to reality, we needed to remind ourselves that much of what is presented us as reality in this culture is not real at all (see chapter 7).

When our desolation expressed itself as sadness, we needed to grieve for the loss of our image of America and find new ways to feel proud of our country (see chapter 8).

When we felt alone, we needed the companionship of our friend Jesus, who was up against the same thing (see chapter 9).

When our desolation expressed itself as feeling small and helpless, we needed to experience our true size as human beings (see chapter 10).

When we feared talking to people who might strongly disagree with us and felt at a loss for words, we needed to learn nonviolent communication (see chapter 11).

And when our desolation whispered to us that we were powerless to do anything, we needed the comfort we find in the words of Walter Wink, "There is no such thing as objective powerlessness. Our belief that we are powerless is a sure sign that we have been duped" (see chapter 14).

When we listened to the story of our desolation each evening, we didn't always understand right away what we needed. We'd try one thing and then another. We knew that we had heard the story and met the underlying need when our desolation diminished, our energy returned and we felt once again in touch with life and hope.

We listened to our consolation as well, and followed St. Ignatius's advice to do more of whatever gives us consolation. For example, one of our greatest consolations was meeting Howard Zinn. We left him feeling profoundly strengthened and encouraged. Reflecting on this later, in the examen, we realized we had felt ourselves in a field of courage while we were in Dr. Zinn's presence. Some of his courage seemed to have come into us, as if it were contagious. This was so noticeable that we took it as a sign of something we should do more of.

During the next few years, we took every possible opportunity to be in the physical presence of courageous people, often traveling great distances to do so. Some of them we already knew in person, while others we knew only by reputation. We wrote to several people we didn't know personally and asked if we could come and talk to them. We also attended conferences or went to meetings where a courageous person we'd never met was speaking. What mattered to us was being in a field of courage and "catching" it. A great many of the quotes and resources in this book came from all these people who gave us courage.

Besides courage, many of these people gave us empathy and unconditional love. As we mentioned in chapter 8, we had learned from Dr. Elisabeth Kübler-Ross that we can move through the stages of dying if we have a significant person who loves us and with whom we can share our feelings at each stage. The same is true for healing any hurt. If we have someone who can receive our feelings without trying to fix or change them in any way, we can take in love right where we are and experience healing.[12]

We began to share what we'd learned and what we were feeling with people we believed we could trust. Occasionally we made mistakes and opened ourselves to people who could not accompany us. Sharing our journey and all that we had learned seemed to frighten, anger or otherwise upset them. These were some of our most painful moments. In general, however, we received the unconditional love and support we needed. We formed a community of people who shared our desire to understand what was happening in our country and to integrate it with spirituality and nonviolence.

In this environment of love and support, we were each able to address our early wounds that had been activated. I (Sheila) used every event that came up in my life during that time to practice trusting my intuition about who was safe and who was not, and to set boundaries that I would not allow to be violated. During my (Denny's) daily jog of several miles through the beautiful mountains around our home, I cared for my fear of scarcity by breathing in the abundance around me. I (Matt) focused on the infinite love and life that really were there in the womb for me and that were more powerful than any violence. It was also important for me to heal my fear of death, in part by developing my awareness of all the people on the other side who care for me.

## Healing Process: Societal Events and Inner Wounds

Our purpose in this chapter is to invite all of us to become aware of whatever in our world disturbs us and of how that may activate inner wounds that we still carry. As we care for those wounds and find ways to meet our underlying needs, we can recover our power to create a better future for ourselves and our children.

(Again, this process is oriented toward Americans. If you are a citizen of another country, we encourage you to adapt it accordingly.)

1. Sit comfortably, close your eyes and place your hand on your heart. Let your awareness go down into your heart and imagine that you are breathing in and out through your heart.
2. Once again recall one or more moments when you felt happy and proud to be an American. For what were you most grateful? How has the United States nurtured and cared for you and your loved ones? Hold your feeling of appreciation for your country in your heart, and let it grow there.
3. Now ask yourself what disturbs you in our society today? What do you see happening around you (or elsewhere in the

world in the name of the United States) that violates your sense of decency, fairness and compassion? Notice how your body reacts to each issue. Which one evokes the strongest reaction within you?

4. Where do you most carry that reaction in your body? Place your hand there and gently care for that part of yourself.
5. Notice whatever feelings come up, and be with them without trying to fix or change them in any way. Follow your feelings and see where they lead you. You might want to ask yourself, "When in the past did I feel this most?" Continue to gently care for yourself, keeping your hand on the part of your body that most carries your feelings.
6. Ask yourself what you most need.

    Perhaps you will want to reexperience a time when you had similar feelings and were able to act on your own behalf in a healthy and constructive way.

    Perhaps your feelings are inviting you in the direction of action in the present. If so, you may want to imagine yourself acting effectively in the situation that concerns you now, and you may want to breathe in whatever resources you need.

    Perhaps you will want to recall a person who loves you or a place where you feel safe and at peace. If so, imagine yourself with that person or in that place.

    Whatever you need, breathe it in for as long as you wish.

## Chapter 14

# THE HEALING POWER OF THE SMALL

Because we are so far from living out Jesus' dream for the future, does that mean both we and Jesus have failed? As if anticipating that his followers might be tempted to think so, Jesus spoke often of inconspicuous beginnings—the small amount of leaven that produces fifty pounds of bread (Matt 13:33), the tiny mustard seed that grows into the largest shrub (Matt 13:31) or the few seeds that land in good soil and produce an astonishing hundredfold yield (Mark 4:1–9).

Archbishop Oscar Romero, who (like Jesus) was killed because he dared to challenge the domination system of El Salvador, understood Jesus' trust in small beginnings. The following prayer, "Prophets of a Future Not Our Own," was written by Ken Untener in 1979, but is commonly known as "Oscar Romero's Prayer":

> It helps, now and then, to step back and take the long view.
> The kingdom is not only beyond our efforts, it is beyond our vision....
> This is what we are about: We plant seeds that one day will grow.
> We water seeds already planted, knowing that they hold future promise.
> We lay foundations that will need further development.

We provide yeast that produces effects beyond our capabilities.
We cannot do everything and there is a sense of liberation in realizing that.
This enables us to do something, and to do it well.
It may be incomplete, but it is a beginning, a step along the way, an opportunity for God's grace to enter and to do the rest.
We may never see the end results, but that is the difference between the master builder and the worker.
We are workers, not master builders, ministers, not messiahs.
We are prophets of a future not our own. Amen.

## Gratitude Is a Sacred Space

In the previous chapter, we focused on the examen process and its emphasis upon returning to moments of consolation, moments when our needs were met and for which we are grateful. The realm described in Oscar Romero's prayer, and in so many of Jesus' sayings, is characterized by gratitude and appreciation for the smallest things, which helps us plant seeds and be prophets of a future not our own. Brother David Steindl-Rast writes,

> ...by counteracting fear, gratefulness reduces and eventually eliminates aggression. By promoting frugality, gratefulness counteracts the prevailing consumerism and its economic underpinnings. And by promoting appreciation of the earth as gratuitous gift, gratefulness counteracts exploitation of Earth's resources and promotes environmental rightness.[1]

Brother David is describing a sacred space in which results don't matter so much as the joy of living in that space, especially if we have companions.

We lived in such an environment of gratitude when we went to Guatemala. We stayed in a small mountain village with the most loving and generous people we had ever met. They made special meals for us from the beans they had grown—three kinds of beans in the same meal rather than the usual one kind—to express their appreciation for us. They gave us their handwoven blankets so we would be warm, even though they might be cold. When we put a stick on the fire in our small house, we knew someone had carried it down the mountain on his or her back. They gave us richly embroidered clothes as gifts when we left, every stitch made by hand.

We left Guatemala so touched by the grateful spirit of these people that we decided to learn Spanish so we could communicate better with them on our next visit. We spent the next several months at a language school in Bolivia, where we went to our classes motivated by love for Hispanic people rather than by wanting to get good grades. We all learned so rapidly that within two months we were giving talks in Spanish at a local church. The more we could communicate with the people, the more we appreciated them and the more we wanted to be with them. We decided to spend most of the next three years giving retreats in Guatemala and all over Latin America. We still work in Mexico for long periods every year, and all our books have been translated into Spanish.

## The Power of the Small

In the sacred space of gratitude, we can plant Oscar Romero's seeds. We can ask, "What gift, however small, do I have that can help this situation?" Often the answer will surprise us. For example, Walter Wink tells the following story:

> This boy was the smallest in his class, and he had chronic sinusitis. His nose was always running. On his school bus there was a bully who was terrorizing everyone. Finally, one day the little kid had had it. Blowing a load of snot into his right hand, he approached the bully, his hand out. "I want to shake the hand of a real bully," he said. The bully backed up until he reached the back of the bus, where he sat down and never bothered anyone again. That nose was always at the ready!
>
> ...the boy found his strength in his greatest weakness. The very thing he hated most about himself had become the source of his power.[2]

This child found a surprising way to protect himself by using the power of the small: a runny nose, which is something most of us regard with disdain.

The people of the village in Guatemala that we love so much did something similar, on a larger scale. During the years we worked there, the Guatemalan army routinely tortured and killed indigenous leaders as a way of maintaining that country's domination system. The villagers saw that when the army invaded a town and took prisoners, they would exploit family feuds in order to gather "information" that a person was helping the guerillas. Then that person, even if innocent, was taken away and tortured (to get more names) and eventually killed. Every town had family feuds and, as long as a town was divided from within, no one was safe.

The villagers asked us to teach them about forgiveness. After we left, they continued forgiving one another until all the ancient family feuds were healed. Now they could all say, "We are one family and we will not allow anyone to divide us." The men began to take turns guarding the entryways to the town. If troops were spotted, the villagers rang the church bell and formed circles around anyone the soldiers wanted to take away. The army could no longer take any prisoners, and this small village of poor, uneducated people became one of the safest places in Guatemala.

In this story and that of the boy with the bully, appreciation for what had previously been despised—a runny nose or hated neighbors—completely changed the dynamics of a violent situation and overcame injustice. Perhaps this is because appreciation and gratitude lead to wonder, and wonder is incompatible with violence. Angie O'Gorman writes that wonder creates a "context of conversion," because the human psyche cannot be in a state of wonder and a state of cruelty simultaneously.[3] Wonder includes surprise. The bully on the bus was so surprised by the boy's unexpected means of self-defense that he backed down. The Guatemalan soldiers were so surprised by the solidarity of the villagers that they left without taking any prisoners.

Just as feelings of appreciation and gratitude create a cascade of positive physical and emotional changes in individuals, so, too, such feelings create a cascade of positive changes in social structures. The smallest things, used by the simplest people in a spirit of gratitude, can change the world.[4a] For example,

[a]Our confidence that this is true rests in part upon the number of successful nonviolent revolutions that have occurred around the world during the past several decades, often involving small actions taken by communities of people in solidarity with one another. One example is the 1986 Philippine Revolution, in which women and children stopped military tanks from firing by offering flowers and food to soldiers. See the DVD series, *A Force More Powerful* (York Zimmerman, 2000), which documents six examples of such actions: Gandhi and the struggle of the Indian people for independence from the British, the rescue of the Jews in Denmark during World War II, the integration of lunch counters in Nashville, TN, during the American Civil Rights movement, Solidarity in Poland, the end of apartheid in South Africa and the overthrow of Pinochet in Chile. Available from www.yorkzim.com.

> In South Africa, prior to the abolition of apartheid, people used to light a candle and place it in their windows as a sign of hope, a sign that one day this evil would be overcome. At one point, this was declared illegal, just as illegal as carrying a gun. Reflecting upon what ultimately brought its demise, it is fair to suggest that "lit candles" (which the government so wisely feared) were considerably more powerful than were guns.[5]

## We Are Never Really Powerless

Fear grows to the extent that we lose our voice and our power and therefore feel helpless and hopeless. Healing comes when we regain our voice and exercise our power. As Walter Wink writes, "There is no such thing as objective powerlessness. Our belief that we are powerless is a sure sign that we have been duped...."[6]

Sometimes we can use our power to make immediate and obvious changes in the outer world. Whether or not that happens, we can always change our own inner world, which in the long run changes the outer world as well. Consider the following story, told by a woman who was hidden from the Nazis as a child:

> One time we hadn't had any food for a while, and all we had left was a limp carrot. A single carrot. It must have been a couple of days old. It was flopping over. It was Chanukah time, and I felt enormous sadness because this was all we had. Had I known what was going on with other Jewish children and families then, I would have considered myself very lucky. All I knew at the time was that we had become like gypsies, constantly on the move with no place that was safe for us. Our clothes were filthy; we couldn't take hot baths or sit down at a table and talk or have any normalcy at all.

That particular night we were hiding in a barn, sleeping on hay. I was feeling sorry for myself. I said to my father, "It's Chanukah. We don't even have a menorah light."

My father said, "What do you mean, we don't have a Chanukah menorah? We have the most beautiful menorah possible!" With that he opened the door a crack, pointed upward, and said, "Look up at the sky." We were someplace in the country. It was pitch-black night, so the stars were brilliant. He said, "Pick out the shammash." (The shammash is the head candle on a menorah.) I picked out the most brilliant star. My father said, "Good. Now let's pick out the other eight candles." So we picked out the other eight candles, and we lit a menorah in the sky.

It was beautiful! So close to heaven and close to God. Then we went back into the barn, and we played with an imaginary dreidel. We were spinning it, and then we'd call out what we got. Not unexpectedly I won! The prize was the carrot—that carrot, which just a few moments before had been a symbol of deprivation and sadness and loss, suddenly became a treasured prize.

Magnanimously I shared that carrot with the whole family. In whispers we sang Chanukah songs, and it felt wonderful to be Jewish. That turned out to be probably the most memorable Chanukah I've ever had, and the most joyous.[7]

Although many holocaust survivors who were hidden from the Nazis as children bear deep emotional scars, this woman is notable for her vibrancy and evident emotional health. Even when gratitude, appreciation and wonder do not seem to outwardly change a situation of injustice, they can empower us to emerge from it whole.

## Infinite Possibility

We wrote this book out of love, because we love John and we dream of a good future for him. How can we fulfill our dreams for ourselves and for those we love? Much of what we have written is about the toxic aspects of our social environment that distract, confuse, entrance and disempower us, convincing us that we are helpless to do anything about the future. Yet, when we remember who we are, we find that what we need is right in front of us, often hidden in something very small, like a runny nose. When we think all we have is a limp carrot, the night sky says, "Have I got a menorah for you!"

When we remember what has given us life, as John did when he wore his old orange soccer jersey, or as Denny did when he recalled joyful family trips from his childhood by taking his father to the field of dreams, we open a door into a realm of love and creativity that is always available to us. Such memories are not just memories of the past; they are reminders that we live in a universe of infinite possibilities that are right there in front of us all the time. Recalling moments when we knew our light, when we knew who we are, connects us with the evolutionary impulse within us that creates what we need in every present moment to heal the future.

> The future is an infinite succession of presents, and to live now as we think human beings should live, in defiance of all that is bad around us, is itself a marvelous victory.
>
> Howard Zinn[8]

## Healing Process: Creating the Future

1. Close your eyes and breathe deeply. Place your hand on your heart and let your attention move from your head down into your heart. Imagine that you are breathing through your heart.
2. As you continue breathing deeply, find someone you carry in your heart whom you love so much that you want to create the best possible future for that person and for yourself. Feel the bond of love between you and that person, and let it grow in your heart.
3. Recall a moment when you were in touch with the realm of infinite possibility that is always available to you. Perhaps you will want to go back to a positive memory you remembered as you read this book. Perhaps you will want to reflect on the first examen question in chapter 12 and ask yourself what you are most grateful for today. Or perhaps some other memory of love feels most alive to you right now.
4. Whatever positive memory moves you most, hold your feeling of appreciation for that moment in your heart and let it grow there.
5. Staying in touch with the love you felt in that moment, dream of the future you want to create for the person you love and for yourself.
6. Is there a way, however small, in which you want to begin to live out your dream?

Appendix

# FEELINGS AND NEEDS

The following lists of feelings and needs were adapted from the Center for Nonviolent Communication Web site, www.cnvc.org.

## Feelings When Your Needs Are Satisfied

| | | |
|---|---|---|
| AFFECTIONATE<br>Compassionate<br>Friendly<br>Loving<br>Openhearted<br>Sympathetic<br>Tender<br>Warm<br><br>ENGAGED<br>Absorbed<br>Alert<br>Curious<br>Engrossed<br>Enchanted<br>Entranced<br>Fascination<br>Interest<br>Intrigued<br>Involved<br>Spellbound<br>Stimulated | HOPEFUL<br>Expectant<br>Encouraged<br>Optimistic<br><br>CONFIDENT<br>Empowered<br>Open<br>Proud<br>Safe<br>Secure<br><br>EXCITEMENT<br>Amazement<br>Animation<br>Ardent<br>Aroused<br>Astonishment<br>Dazzled<br>Eager<br>Energetic<br>Enthusiastic<br>Giddy | Invigoration<br>Lively<br>Passionate<br>Surprise<br>Vibrant<br><br>GRATEFUL<br>Appreciative<br>Moved<br>Thankful<br>Touched<br><br>INSPIRED<br>Amazed<br>Awed<br>Wonder<br><br>JOYFUL<br>Amused<br>Delight<br>Glad<br>Happy<br>Jubilant |

| | | |
|---|---|---|
| Pleased | PEACEFUL | Serene |
| Tickled | Calm | Still |
| EXHILARATED | Clearheaded | Tranquil |
| Blissful | Comfortable | Trusting |
| Ecstatic | Centered | REFRESHED |
| Elated | Content | Enlivened |
| Enthralled | Fulfilled | Rejuvenated |
| Exuberant | Mellow | Renewed |
| Radiant | Quiet | Rested |
| Rapturous | Relaxation | Restored |
| Thrilled | Relief | Revived |
| | Satisfaction | |

## Feelings When Your Needs Are Not Satisfied

| | | |
|---|---|---|
| AFRAID | Frustration | Hostile |
| Apprehensive | Impatient | Repulsion |
| Dread | Irritation | CONFUSION |
| Foreboding | ANGRY | Ambivalent |
| Fright | Enraged | Baffled |
| Mistrustful | Furious | Bewildered |
| Panic | Indignant | Dazed |
| Petrified | Irate | Hesitant |
| Scared | Livid | Lost |
| Suspicious | Outrage | Mystified |
| Terror | Resentful | Perplexed |
| Wary | AVERSION | Puzzled |
| Worried | Animosity | Torn |
| ANNOYANCE | Contempt | DISCONNECTION |
| Aggravation | Disgust | Alienation |
| Dismay | Dislike | Aloof |
| Disgruntlement | Hate | Apathetic |
| Displeasure | Horror | Boredom |
| Exasperation | | |

Cold
Detached
Disinterest
Distant
Distraction
Indifferent
Numb
Withdrawn

DISQUIET
Agitation
Alarmed
Discombobulated
Disturbance
Perturbation
Restless
Shock
Startled
Surprise
Troubled
Turbulent
Turmoil
Uncomfortable
Uneasy
Unnerved
Unsettled
Upset

EMBARRASSMENT
Chagrin
Flustered
Guilty
Mortification
Self-conscious
Shame

FATIGUE
Beat
Burnt-out
Depleted
Exhausted
Lethargic
Listless
Sleepy
Tired
Weary
Worn out

PAIN
Agony
Anguish
Bereaved
Devastated
Grief
Heartbroken
Hurt
Lonely
Miserable
Regretful
Remorseful

SAD
Depression
Dejection
Despair
Despondent
Disappointment
Discouragment
Disheartened
Forlorn
Gloomy
Heavyhearted
Hopeless

Melancholy
Unhappy
Wretched

TENSE
Anxious
Cranky
Distress
Distraught
Edgy
Fidgety
Frazzled
Irritable
Jittery
Nervous
Overwhelmed
Restless
Stressed out

VULNERABLE
Fragile
Guarded
Helpless
Insecure
Leery
Reserved
Sensitive
Shaky

YEARNING
Envious
Jealous
Longing
Nostalgic
Pining
Wistful

## Needs

| CONNECTION | PHYSICAL WELL-BEING | MEANING |
|---|---|---|
| Acceptance | Air | Awareness |
| Affection | Food | Celebration of life |
| Appreciation | Movement/exercise | Challenge |
| Belonging | Rest/sleep | Clarity |
| Cooperation | Sexual expression | Competence |
| Communication | Safety | Consciousness |
| Closeness | Shelter | Contribution |
| Community | Touch | Creativity |
| Companionship | Water | Discovery |
| Compassion | **HONESTY** | Efficacy |
| Consideration | Authenticity | Effectiveness |
| Consistency | Integrity | Growth |
| Empathy | Presence | Hope |
| Inclusion | **PLAY** | Learning |
| Intimacy | Joy | Mourning |
| Love | Humor | Participation |
| Mutuality | **PEACE** | Purpose |
| Nurturing | Beauty | Self-expression |
| Respect/self-respect | Communion | Stimulation |
| Safety | Ease | To matter |
| Security | Equality | Understanding |
| Stability | Harmony | |
| Support | Inspiration | |
| To know and be known | Order | |
| To see and be seen | **AUTONOMY** | |
| To understand and be understood | Choice | |
| Trust | Freedom | |
| Warmth | Independence | |
| | Space | |
| | Spontaneity | |

# NOTES

## Introduction: Musical Chairs

1. Howard Zinn, "The Optimism of Uncertainty," http://www.thenation.com/doc/20040920/zinn, September 2, 2004 (accessed August 27, 2010).

2. We are indebted to Terry Orlick for the cooperative way of playing musical chairs. This is only one of hundreds of noncompetitive games collected in Terry Orlick, *The Cooperative Sports and Games Book* (New York: Pantheon, 1978), and *The Second Cooperative Sports and Games Book* (New York: Pantheon, 1982).

3. Sheila Fabricant Linn, Dennis Linn and Matthew Linn, *Healing Our Beginning* (New York/Mahwah, NJ: Paulist Press, 2005).

4. Walter Wink, "Toward a Social Psychology of Domination," presentation to the Society of Biblical Literature (Psychology and Biblical Studies Section), San Francisco, 1992, under the title, "Who Is Like the Beast? (Rev 12—13): Toward a Social Psychology of Domination," 1. Similar ideas appear in Walter Wink, *Engaging the Powers: Discernment and Resistance in a World of Domination* (Minneapolis: Fortress, 1992), chapter 5.

5. Matthew Linn, Sheila Fabricant Linn and Dennis Linn, *Healing the Eight Stages of Life* (New York/Mahwah, NJ: Paulist Press, 1988).

6. James O'Dea, "You Were Born for the Challenge of This Epoch," presentation at the Science and Consciousness Conference, Santa Fe, NM, April, 2007.

## Chapter 1: Remembering Who We Are

1. This picture can be found in Jennifer Morgan, *Mammals Who Morph: The Universe Tells Our Evolution Story* (Nevada City, CA: Dawn Publications, 2006), 43. Also available at http://map.gsfc.nasa.gov/media/101080/index.html (accessed August 27, 2010).

For extensive resources on the new story of the universe and the implications of our being made of stardust, including resources for children, see the educational Web site maintained by Connie Barlow and Michael Dowd, www.thegreatstory.org. For the new story integrated with spirituality, see Michael Dowd, *Thank God for Evolution!: How the Marriage of Science and Religion Will Transform Your Life and Our World* (New York: Plume/Penguin, 2009); Michael Morwood, *Praying a New Story* (Maryknoll, NY: Orbis, 2004), and *Children Praying a New Story* (South Bend, IN: Kelmore, 2009).

2. David Bohm, *Wholeness and the Implicate Order* (London: Routledge and Kegan Paul, 1980).

3. Pim van Lommel, *Consciousness Beyond Life: The Science of the Near-Death Experience* (New York: HarperCollins, 2010), front cover flap.

4. For the effects of near-death experiences, see van Lommel, *Consciousness Beyond Life*, 68; Melvin Morse, *Transformed by the Light* (New York: Ivy Books, 1992), 158–59, 163–65, 204–5 and 213; Kenneth Ring, *Life at Death: A Scientific Investigation of the Near-Death Experience* (New York: William Morrow, 1982), and *Heading Toward Omega* (San Francisco: Harper, 1985).

## Chapter 2: Positive Memories: Find the Orange Shirt

1. Doc Childre and Howard Martin, *The HeartMath Solution* (San Francisco: Harper, 1999), 38–40; Jurriaan Kamp, "A

Change of Heart Changes Everything," *Ode* (June, 2005): 25. For the most current HeartMath research, see www.Heartmath.org/research (accessed August 27, 2010).

2. Bruce H. Lipton, "Embracing the Immaterial Universe," *Shift* 9 (December, 2005–February, 2006): 12.

3. *Science Daily*, "Brain Scans of the Future: Psychologists Use FMRI to Understand Ties Between Memories and the Imagination" (July 1, 2007), www.sciencedaily.com/videos/2007/0710-brain_scans_of_the_future.htm?sms_ss=em (accessed February 7, 2011).

4. *Pass It On* (New York: Alcoholics Anonymous World Services, 1984), 56. For a more complete discussion of the relationship between positive memories and recovery from addictions, see Dennis Linn, Sheila Fabricant Linn and Matthew Linn, *Belonging: Bonds of Healing and Recovery* (New York/Mahwah, NJ: Paulist Press, 1993), 7–17.

5. *Twelve Steps and Twelve Traditions* (New York: Alcoholics Anonymous World Services, 1953), 105.

6. *Alcoholics Anonymous* (New York: Alcoholics Anonymous World Services, 1976), 84–85.

7. Miller Farms, 9040 U.S. Highway 66, Platteville CO 80651, (970) 785-6133, www.millerfarms.net (accessed February 7, 2011). Although Miller Farms is not certified as organic, they use organic farming methods.

8. The SAME Café, 2023 E. Colfax Ave., Denver CO, (720) 530-6853, www.soallmayeat.org (accessed February 1, 2011).

9. Neil Douglas-Klotz audio program "The Healing Breath" (Boulder, CO: Sounds True, 2004).

10. Bruce Lipton, *The Biology of Belief* (New York: Hay House, 2008), 155. See also p. 15.

11. Matthew Fox and Rupert Sheldrake, *Natural Grace* (Garden City, NY: Image, 1997), 99.

12. Kamp, "A Change of Heart Changes Everything," 22–27.

13. L. Song, G. Schwartz and L. Russek, "Heart-Focused Attention and Heart-Brain Synchronization: Energetic and Physiological Mechanisms, Alternative Therapies," *Health and Medicine* 4:5 (1998): 44–62, cited in Childre and Martin, *The HeartMath Solution,* 33. See also www.heartmath.org/research.

14. Childre and Martin, *The HeartMath Solution*, 28–34 and ff. See also www.heartmath.org/research.

15. Ibid., 33–34; Kamp, "A Change of Heart Changes Everything," 22–27. See also www.heartmath.org/research.

16. See www.heartmath.org/research. For research on treating ADD/ADHD in children, see Shari St. Martin, Biofeedback Clinic, Guadalajara, Jalisco, Mexico, "The Garden of the Heart: The New Biotechnology for Treating Children with ADD/ADHD and Arrhythmia," www.heartmath.org/research/rp-garden-of-the-heart-heartmath-the-new-biotechnology-for-treating-children-with-add/adhd.html (accessed August 28, 2010).

17. Childre and Martin, *The HeartMath Solution*, 248; Kamp, "A Change of Heart Changes Everything," 25, 26; R. McCraty et al., "The Impact of a New Emotional Self-Management Program on Stress, Emotions, Heart Rate Variability, DHEA and Cortisol," *Integrative Physiological and Behavioral Science* 33:2 (April–June, 1998): 151–70. See also www.heartmath.org/research.

This healing effect of appreciation and gratitude extends far into the future. Harvard's Dr. George Valiant asked, "How can one predict among 50-year-olds who would age happily and well and who would become sad and sick?" His sixty-year study found six predictors (a stable marriage, no smoking, little use of alcohol, regular exercise, maintenance of normal weight and a mature adaptive style) of who at eighty would be among "happy-well" as opposed to "sad-sick." The most powerful predictor of successful aging was consistently using "a mature adaptive style" marked by gratitude and forgiveness (*Spirituality and Health* [Fall, 2001]: 15).

## Chapter 3: Competition

1. Alfie Kohn, *No Contest: The Case Against Competition* (Boston: Houghton Mifflin, 1986), 147.

2. Annie Leonard, "The Story of Stuff," www.storyofstuff.com (accessed August 29, 2010).

3. Leonardo Boff, "Sustainable Retreat," November 16, 2007, http://leonardoboff.com/site-eng/lboff.htm (accessed August 27, 2010).

4. Ibid.

5. Lipton, "Embracing the Immaterial Universe," 10.

6. Paul H. Ray and Sherry Ruth Anderson, *The Cultural Creatives: How 50 Million People are Changing the World* (New York: Harmony Books, 2000), 4.

7. Ibid.

8. Paul Hawken, *Blessed Unrest: How the Largest Movement in the World Came into Being and Why No One Saw It Coming* (New York: Viking, 2007), front cover flap. See also a brief and inspiring video summary at http://www.blessedunrest.com/video.html (accessed February 7, 2011).

9. Jurriaan Kamp and Marco Visscher, "Turning Poverty into Peace," *Ode* 4:10 (December, 2006): 40–49. The nonprofit model of microlending developed by Yunus and his Grameen Bank is based upon keeping money and interest income in the local community. Some subsequent microcredit programs have not replicated this essential component of the Grameen Bank model. They have instead become for-profit enterprises that rely on foreign investment and may ultimately serve the rich at the expense of the poor. See David Korten, "Microcredit: The Good, the Bad and the Ugly: Unraveling the Confusion Behind Microcredit: How Some Models

Help Alleviate Poverty, While Others Exploit the Poor to Make the Rich Richer," *YES! Magazine* (January 20, 2011), http://www.comondreams.org/ print/64630 (accessed January 22, 2011).

10. Janet Paskin, "Think Outside the Bank," *Ode* 5:10 (December, 2007): 38–39. As of February 7, 2011, 552,277 people in 210 countries have funded loans totaling $191,298,525 for 496,477 people, with an average repayment rate of 98.92 percent.

11. Hawken, *Blessed Unrest,* 184.

12. Ibid., 165.

13. Caitlin Weaver, "The Great 3,100-Mile Foot Race," *Ode* 5:9 (November 24, 2007): 28, www.selftranscendence.org/3100_mile_race (accessed August 27, 2010).

14. Lillian Rubin, *Just Friends: The Role of Friendship in Our Lives* (New York: Harper & Row, 1985), 81–82, cited in Kohn, *No Contest*, 35.

15. Bruce Ogilvie and Thomas Tutko, "Sport: If You Want to Build Character, Try Something Else," *Psychology Today* (October, 1971): 61–63, cited in Kohn, *No Contest*, 134.

16. O. Fred Donaldson, "Belonging: That Bargain Struck in Child's Play," *ReVision* 17:4 (Spring, 1995): 29.

17. Kohn, *No Contest*, 44.

18. Ibid.

19. Michael B. Quanty, "Aggression Catharsis: Experimental Investigations and Implications," in Russell G. Geen and Edgar C. O'Neal, eds., *Perspectives on Aggression* (New York: Academic Press, 1976), 117–18, cited in Kohn, *No Contest*, 144.

20. Richard G. Sipes, "War, Sports and Aggression: An Empirical Test of Two Rival Theories," *American Anthropologist* 75 (1973): 71, cited in Kohn, *No Contest*, 144.

21. From the DVD series by Ken Burns, *Baseball, Inning Eight: 1960–1970*, no. 13: "Pondering Inaction." Carlin notes that, in contrast to football, in baseball the object is "to go home…to be safe at home."

22. Gary Warner, *Competition* (Elgin, IL: David C. Cook, 1979), 171, cited in Kohn, *No Contest*, 145.

23. John Long, Silvana Q. Montanaro and Jane M. Healy, "The Technology Screen," *AMI/USA: Parenting for a New World* 12:4 (December, 2003); Jerry Mander, *Four Arguments for the Elimination of Television* (New York: HarperCollins, 1977); Linda S. Pagani, Caroline Fitzpatrick, Tracie A. Barnett and Eric Dubow, "Associations Between Early Childhood Television Exposure and Academic, Psychosocial and Physical Well-Being by Middle Childhood," *Archives of Pediatrics and Adolescent Medicine* 164:5 (May, 2010): 425–31, cited in Rachael Rettner, "Watching TV at Age 2 Linked to a Host of Problems at 10," http://news.yahoo.com/s/livescience/watchingtvatage2linkedtoahostofproblemsat10 (accessed May 3, 2010); Jeanna Bryner, "TV Causes Learning Lag in Infants," June 1, 2009, http://news.yahoo.com/s/livescience/20090601/sc_livescience/tvcauseslearninglagininfants/ (accessed June 3, 2009); American Academy of Pediatrics Committee on Public Education, Policy Statement, "Children, Adolescents, and Television," *Pediatrics* 107:2 (February, 2001): 423–26, http://aappolicy.aappublications.org/cgi/content/full/pediatrics;107/2/4 23 (accessed August 27, 2010); Aric Sigman, "How TV Is (Quite Literally) Killing Us," *Daily Mail* (October 1, 2005), http://www.whale.to/b/sigman.html (accessed February 5, 2011).

24. O. Fred Donaldson, *Playing by Heart* (Deerfield Beach, FL: Health Communications, 1993), 193. Used with permission.

25. Orlick, *The Cooperative Sports and Games Book* and *The Second Cooperative Sports and Games Book*.

26. Orlick, *The Cooperative Sports and Games Book*, 52.

27. Hawken, *Blessed Unrest*, 186–87; James Carse, *Finite and Infinite Games: A Vision of Life as Play and Possibility* (New York: Ballantine, 1986).

## Chapter 4: Punishment

1. *As Bill Sees It* (New York: Alcoholics Anonymous World Services, 1967), 98.

2. Lt. Col. Dave Grossman, *On Killing: The Psychological Cost of Learning to Kill in War and Society* (New York: Little, Brown & Co., 1995).

3. Grossman, *On Killing,* 180; Martha Stout, *The Sociopath Next Door* (New York: Broadway Books, 2005), 6.

4. Grossman, *On Killing,* xiv–xv, 3–4, 12, 15, 17–25, 35, 180.

5. S. L. A. Marshall, *Men Against Fire* (Gloucester, MA: Peter Smith, 1978), 50, 54, cited in Alfie Kohn, *The Brighter Side of Human Nature* (New York: Basic Books, 1990), 49.

6. Kohn, *Brighter Side,* 49–50.

7. Marshall, *Men Against Fire*, 78–79; see also 59; cited in Kohn, *Brighter Side,* 50.

8. Grossman, *On Killing*, 160–61, 249–61, 306–11.

9. Ibid., 302–3, 314–16; Jamie Holmes, "U.S. Military Is Meeting Recruitment Goals with Video Games—But at What Cost?" *The Christian Science Monitor,* December 28, 2009; Camillo Bica, "Deadly Games," www.truth-out.org/050509J (accessed August 28, 2010); Avril Moore, "War Is No Game, So Why Is It Marketed to Children as One?" *Sydney Morning Herald*, June 15, 2010, http://www.smh.com.au/opinion/society-and-culture/war-is-no-game-so-why-is-it-marketed-to-children-as-one-20100614-ya3d.html (accessed August 28, 2010).

10. Grossman, *On Killing*, 35, 181, 250, 251.

11. Film by David Zeiger, *Sir! No Sir!* www.sirnosir.com (accessed August 27, 2010). Although the draft army of the Vietnam era is gone and we now have an all-volunteer army, acts of resistance persist. See Dahr Jamail, "Refusing to Comply: The Tactics of Resistance in an All-Volunteer Military," June 30, 2009, http://www.truth-out.org/070109K (accessed February 6, 2011).

12. Grossman, *On Killing*, 281–89. The number of military hospitalizations for injuries in 2009 was 11,156, whereas the number of military hospitalizations for mental health issues in that same year was 17,538. Gregg Zoroya, *USA Today*, May 14, 2010, cited in *Yes! Magazine* (Fall, 2010): 16.

13. *The Christmas Truce*, DVD produced by the History Channel, 2002; *Joyeaux Noel*, film produced by Alexandre Lippens et al., 2002; Paul Magnarella, "The Christmas Truce of 1914," www.truth-out.org/122409Magnarella (accessed August 27, 2010); children's book by John McCutcheon, *Christmas in the Trenches* (Atlanta: Peachtree, 2006); includes a CD with two songs about the Christmas truce and a reading of the story; Stanley Weintraub, *Silent Night: The Remarkable Christmas Truce of 1914* (New York: Pocket, 2002).

14. Jeremy Rivkin, *The Empathic Civilization: The Race to Global Consciousness in a World in Crisis* (New York: Jeremy P. Tarcher/Penguin, 2009), 82–84. For a delightful animated ten-minute video summary of this book, see http://www.youtube.com/watch?v=l7AWnfFRc7g&feature=player_embedded (accessed February 14, 2011). See also Maia Szalavitz and Bruce D. Perry, *Born for Love: Why Empathy Is Essential—and Endangered* (New York: HarperCollins, 2010), 21–22; G. Rizzolatti and C. Sinigaglia, *Mirrors in the Brain: How Our Minds Share Actions and Emotions* (New York: Oxford University Press, 2008); M. Iacoboni, *Mirroring People: The New Science of How We Connect with Others* (New York: Farrar, Straus & Giroux, 2009), 110; T. Singer et al., "Empathy for Pain Involves the Affective but Not Sensory Components of Pain," *Science* 303:5661 (February 20, 2004): 1157–62, cited in Szalavitz and Perry, *Born for Love*.

15. Shankar Vedantam, "If It Feels Good to Be Good, It Might Be Only Natural," *Washington Post*, May 28, 2007, http://www.washingtonpost.com/wp-dyn/content/article/2007/05/27/AR2007052701056.html (accessed May 28, 2010).

16. Rivkin, *Empathic Civilization*, 96–104.

17. Randy James, "Child Psychology: A New Look inside Babies' Minds," *Time*, August 14, 2009, http://www.time.com/time/nation/article/0,8599,1916406,00.html (accessed September 4, 2010).

18. Rivkin, *Empathic Civilization*, 131.

19. Ibid., 86. In support of the idea that, although we are predisposed to empathy and altruism, it must be supported by the environment, researchers have found that "even brief exposure to other individuals' prosocial behavior motivates altruism." *Greater Good*, March 1, 2010, http://greatergood.berkeley.edu/article/item/scientific_proof_for_paying_it_forward/.

20. James Prescott, "Body Pleasure and the Origins of Violence," *The Futurist* 9:2 (April, 1975): 73–74, cited by Richard Heinberg in *Museletter* 58 (October, 1996), http://www.richardheinberg.com/ (accessed February 8, 2011) and http://www.postcarbon.org/ (accessed February 8, 2011).

21. *Prescott*, "Body Pleasure," 64–74.

22. Gary Olson, "Research on Human Nature Is Cause for Optimism," *The Morning Call*, June 29, 2007.

23. David Loye, "Darwin's Lost Theory and the Hidden Crisis in Western Education," in Riane Eisler and Ron Miller, eds., *Educating for a Culture of Peace* (Portsmouth, NH: Heinemann, 2004), 42–55; David Loye, "The Ghost at the Birthday Party," CommonDreams.org, February 12, 2009, http://www.commondreams.org/view/2009/02/12-10 (accessed February 8, 2011). See also Rivkin, *Empathic Civilization*, 90–92.

24. William Peters, *A Class Divided: Then and Now*, expanded edition (New Haven: Yale University Press, 1971). Includes an account of Jane Elliott conducting a similar experiment for adult employees of the Iowa Department of Corrections. See also documentary films, *The Eye of the Storm*, ABC News, 1970, distributed in DVD format by Admire Productions, 2004,

www.admireentertainment.com, and *A Class Divided*, by Yale University Films, 1986, presented on *Frontline* and distributed in DVD format by PBS Home Video, www.pbs.org. Both programs include study guides for use with groups.

25. Peters, *A Class Divided*, 21.

26. Ibid., 24–25.

27. Ibid., 109–10.

28. Willis Harman, "Biology Revisioned," *IONS: Noetic Sciences Review* 41 (Spring, 1997): 14.

29. Iacoboni is quoted in Michael Nagler, "The Cassandra Syndrome," April 14, 2009, http://www.truth-out.org/041409L (accessed May 6, 2009).

30. Diarmuid O'Murchu, *Ancestral Grace* (Maryknoll, NY: Orbis, 2008), 6–90; quote is from p. 8.

31. Alfie Kohn, "Punished by Rewards," audio presentation. See also Alfie Kohn, *Unconditional Parenting: Moving from Rewards and Punishment to Love and Reason* (New York: Atria Books, 2005), and his DVD program by the same title, available from www.unconditional parenting.com.

32. Bernard Häring, *Free and Faithful in Christ*, vol. 1 (Slough, UK: St. Paul Publications, 1978), 2.

33. Samuel P. Oliner and Pearl M. Oliner, *The Altruistic Personality: Rescuers of Jews in Nazi Europe* (New York: Macmillan, 1988), 249–50.

## Chapter 5: Rewards

1. Alfie Kohn, *Punished by Rewards: The Trouble with Gold Stars, Incentive Plans, A's, Praise and Other Bribes* (Boston: Houghton Mifflin, 1993).

2. Another example is an experiment that was done in 1973 at blood banks in Kansas City and Denver. One group of people was sent a standard form letter announcing a blood drive. Another

group was sent the same letter, but they were offered money to pay them for donating blood. Ninety-three percent of the first group was willing to donate blood, while only 65 percent of those who were offered money were willing to donate blood. This research demonstrated that the desire to contribute to the common good by offering blood was diminished in a significant number of people if they were offered a cash reward (Jeremy Mercer, "Getting to the Heart of Money," *Ode* 7:4 [May, 2009]: 32).

3. John Nicholls, quoted in Kohn, *Punished by Rewards*, 73. See also 11, 65–66, 73–74.

4. We are indebted to Marshall Rosenberg for his distinction between giving compliments and expressing appreciation. See Rosenberg, *Nonviolent Communication: A Language of Compassion* (DelMar, CA: PuddleDancer Press, 1999), 141–47.

5. Edward L. Deci and Richard M. Ryan, *Intrinsic Motivation and Self-Determination in Human Behavior* (New York: Plenum, 1985), 70, cited in Kohn, *Punished by Rewards*, 26.

6. Kohn, *Punished by Rewards*, 76. For a discussion of how rewards diminish the intrinsic motivation to learn, see also chapters 5 and 8.

7. Ibid., 71–72.

## Chapter 6: Someone Has to Pay

1. Alice Miller, *Banished Knowledge* (New York: Doubleday, 1990), 33, 35. The harmful effects of spanking children have been well documented. One of the most recent carefully researched and widely reported studies, known as the "Tulane Study," is (Catherine A. Taylor, et al.) "Mothers' Spanking of 3-Year-Old Children and Subsequent Risk of Children's Aggressive Behavior," *Pediatrics*, 10.1542/peds.2009-2678 (April 12, 2010), http://pediatrics.aappublications.org/cgi/content/abstract/peds.2009-2678v1 (accessed August 28, 2010). This study was the first to control for a

wide variety of factors that might be related to aggression in children, such as spousal abuse, maternal depression, substance abuse and whether the mother considered abortion during the pregnancy. After controlling for these factors, Taylor found that "The odds of a child being more aggressive at age 5 increased by 50% if he had been spanked more than twice in the month before the study began." Reported in Alice Park, "The Long-Term Effects of Spanking," www.time.com, May 23, 2010, http://www.time.com/time/magazine/article/0,9171,1983895,00.html#ixzz0xwRQHsht (accessed August 28, 2010). See also, for example, Serena Gordon, "Spanking May Lower Kids' IQs," *HealthDay News*, September 25, 2009 (accessed February 6, 2012, at http://health.usnews.com/health-news/family-health/brain-and-behavior/articles/2009/09/25/spanking-may-lower-kids-iqs.) Note that the American Academy of Pediatrics does not endorse spanking under any circumstances.

2. Cited in Walter Wink, *Engaging the Powers* (Minneapolis: Fortress, 1992), 146.

3. Tom Engelhardt, "Hearing Voices, Smiting Enemies," TomDispatch.com, June 26, 2003, http://www.tomdispatch.com/post/781/hearing_voices_smiting_enemies (accessed August 31, 2010).

4. Newsweek poll, reported in Newsweek, May 24, 2004.

5. John Dear, *Transfiguration* (New York: Doubleday, 2007), 30.

6. John Dear, "Letter: War Is Not the Will of God," www.johndear.org, 1.

7. Survey of 742 American adults, conducted on April 14–21, 2009, by the Pew Research Center. Reported in "Survey: Support for Terror Suspect Torture Differs among the Faithful," www.cnn.com/2009/US/04/30/religion.torture/ (accessed August 27, 2010). Forty-nine percent of all respondents, and 54 percent of those who attend church at least once a week, said that "torture

against suspected terrorists in order to gain important information" is "often or sometimes justified." For an excellent commentary on the incongruity of Christianity and torture, see Rich Lang, "Torture: The Continual Crucifixion of Christ," sermon preached at Trinity United Methodist Church, Seattle, July 13, 2008, http://rugerac.blogspot.com/2008/07/torture-continual-crucifixion-of-christ.html (accessed September 6, 2010).

8. Susan Brooks Thistlethwaite, "Why the Faithful Approve of Torture," *Washington Post*, May 1, 2009.

9. Walter Imbiorski, quoted in Dick Westley, *Redemptive Intimacy: A New Perspective for the Journey to Adult Faith* (Mystic CT: Twenty-Third Publications, 1981), 111–12.

10. Richard McBrien, *Catholicism* (San Francisco: Harper, 1994), 482–83.

11. Westley, *Redemptive Intimacy*, 112ff.

12. Donald Senior, CP, "Blame the Gospels," *Commonweal* (May 7, 2004): 17.

13. Joseph Campbell with Bill Moyers, *The Power of Myth* (New York: Doubleday, 1988), 112.

14. Daniel Harrington, SJ, *The Gospel of Matthew* (Collegeville, MN: Liturgical Press, 1991), 283–85.

15. Wink, *Engaging the Powers*, 209.

## Chapter 7: The Trance

1. Barrie Zwicker, *Towers of Deception* (Gabriola Island, BC, Canada: New Society Publishers, 2006), 283.

2. Ibid.

3. Douglas Rushkoff, *Coercion: Why We Listen to What "They" Say* (New York: Penguin, 1999), 64, cited in Kevin Barrett, "Apocalypse of Coercion," http://mujca.com/apocalypse.htm (accessed September 6, 2010).

4. Robert F. Kennedy, Jr., "Eighty Percent of Republicans Are Democrats That Don't Know What's Going On," presentation in New York City, May 2, 2004, http://openpdf.com/ebook/mad house-pdf.html (accessed May 15, 2010).

5. Joel Andreas, *Addicted to War: Why the U.S. Can't Kick Militarism* (Oakland, CA: AK Press, 2004), 58.

6. Ibid., 59.

7. Dave McGowan, *Derailing Democracy: The America the Media Don't Want You to See* (Monroe, ME: Common Courage Press, 2000), 13. See also Carl Bernstein, "The CIA and the Media," *Rolling Stone* (October 20, 1977), http://tmh.floonet.net/articles/cia_press.html (accessed August 31, 2010); Noam Chomsky, audio CD, "Propaganda and Control of the Public Mind" (Oakland, CA: AK Press, 1998).

8. John Pilger, "Flying the Flag, Faking the News," *The New Statesman* (September 2, 2010), http://www.commondreams.org/view/2010/09/02-9 (accessed February 8, 2011).

9. Lipton, "How Your Beliefs Control Your Biology."

10. Kennedy, "Eighty Percent of Republicans Are Democrats That Don't Know What's Going On."

11. Michael Pollan, *In Defense of Food: An Eater's Manifesto* (New York: Penguin, 2008), 1 and ff.

## Chapter 8: Grieving Can Help Us Tell the Truth

1. Michael B. Russell, "Blessed Are Those Who Mourn," *Sojourners* (January 26, 1982): 24–26.

2. Joanna Macy, *Despair and Personal Power in the Nuclear Age* (Philadelphia: New Society Publishers, 1983).

3. David Ray Griffin, "9/11 and Nationalist Faith: How Faith Can Be Illuminating or Blinding," presentation at Iliff School of Theology, Denver, CO, October 19, 2007, http://david raygriffin.

com/lectures/911-and-nationalist-faith/ (accessed August 29, 2010).

4. Joanna Macy, "The Story of the Elm Dance," 3, http://www.joannamacy.net/html/elmdance/storyelm.html (accessed February 20, 2008).

5. Our friends of Norwegian descent confirmed what we had learned from the film clip, "Norway," by Michael Moore (filmed for but not included in his movie, *Sicko*), available at http://www.slashfilm.com/2007/11/22/norway-a-deleted-scene-from-michael-moores-sicko/ (accessed August 28, 2010).

6. David Weiss, "Prison Walls Couldn't Keep Inmates from Lending a Hand," www.prisoners.com/leader (accessed August 24, 2010).

7. Madhu Suri Prakash, "Why the Kings of Bhutan Ride Bicycles," *Yes! Magazine* (January 14, 2011), http://www.yesmagazine.org/issues/what-happy-families-know/why-the-kings-of-bhutan-ride-bicycles (accessed February 12, 2011).

8. Wikipedia, "Capital Punishment," 2006, http://en.wikipedia.org/wiki/Capital_punishment (accessed August 28, 2010). The number of executions carried out in the United States has diminished in recent years, but it remains high in comparison with other countries. Warren Richey, "Death Penalty Less Common in US Now Than in 1990s, Report Finds," December 21, 2010, http://www.truth-out.org/print/66145 (accessed January 23, 2011).

9. Roy Walmsley, *World Prison Population List* (London: Kings College, 8th ed., 2009), http://www.kcl.ac.uk/depsta/law/research/icps/downloads/wppl-8th_41.pdf (accessed August 30, 2010). The United States has 5 percent of the world's population and 25 percent of the world's prisoners (Joseph A. Califano, "Criminally Unjust," *America* [May 14, 2010], http://www.americamagazine.org/content/article.cfm?article_id=12311 [accessed February 8, 2011]).

10. "Endangered Species," library.thinkquest.org/19689/data/esframe (accessed August 24, 2010).

11. Regarding aspartame and MSG, see Russell Blaylock, MD, *Excitotoxins: The Taste That Kills* (Albuquerque, NM: Health Press, 1996). Summarized in Russell Blaylock, "Excitotoxins—The Taste That Kills," http://insuranceandwellness.com/Excitotoxins (accessed August 28, 2010). See also "Donald Rumsfeld and Aspartame," www.newswithviews.com/NWV exclusive/exclusive 15.htm, May 9, 2004 (accessed August 26, 2010); Joseph Mercola, "Aspartame's Dangers, Side Effects and FDA Approval Explained," http://articles.mercola.com/sites/articles/archive/2010/07/31/aspartame-update.aspx (accessed September 15, 2010); Joseph Mercola, "Why This Toxic Sweetener is Far Worse than High Fructose Corn Syrup," http://articles.mercola.com/sites/articles/archive/2010/09/15/aspartame-side-effects.aspx (accessed September 15, 2010).

Film by Cori Brackett, *Sweet Misery: A Poisoned World*, Cinema Libre Distribution, 2005; can be watched online at http://topdocumentaryfilms.com/sweet-misery-a-poisoned-world/ (accessed February 8, 2011).

Regarding genetically modified (or genetically engineered) foods, known as "GM," "GMO" or "GE" foods, see Andrew Kimbrell, *Your Right to Know: Genetic Engineering and the Secret Changes in Your Food* (San Rafael, CA: Earth Aware, 2007); Jeffrey M. Smith, *Seeds of Deception: Exposing Industry and Government Lies About the Safety of the Genetically Engineered Foods You're Eating* (Fairfield, IA: Yes! Books, 2003), and *Genetic Roulette: The Documented Health Risks of Genetically Engineered Foods* (White River Jct., VT: Chelsea Green, 2007 ), www. geneticroulette.com (accessed August 28, 2010); Gilles-Eric Seralini et al., "How Subchronic and Chronic Health Effects Can Be Neglected for GMOs, Pesticides or Chemicals," *International Journal of Biological Sciences* 5 (2009): 438–43; Rady Ananda, "Three Approved

GMO's Linked to Organ Damage," www.truth-out.org/article/three-approved-gmos-linked-organ-damage, January 8, 2010 (accessed August 28, 2010); Byron Richards, "Health Scandal of the Decade—Monsanto's GMO Perversion of Food," www.wellnessresources.com/main/printable/health_scandal_of_the_decade_monsantos_gmo_perversion_of_food, January 19, 2010; Jeffrey M. Smith, "Doctors Warn: Avoid Genetically Modified Food," http://www.seedsofdeception.com/utility/showArticle/?objectID=2989 (accessed February 5, 2011). Citing Netherwood et al., "Assessing the Survival of Trangenic Plant DNA in the Human Gastrointestinal Tract," *Nature Biotechnology* 22 (2004): 2, Smith uses the example of soy to describe what may be most dangerous about GM foods:

> The gene inserted into GM soy transfers into the DNA of bacteria living inside our intestines and *continues to function*. This means that long after we stop eating GMOs, we may still have potentially harmful GM proteins produced continuously inside of us. Put more plainly, eating a corn chip produced from Bt corn might transform our intestinal bacteria into living pesticide factories, possibly for the rest of our lives.
>
> When evidence of gene transfer is reported at medical conferences around the U.S., doctors often respond by citing the huge increase of gastrointestinal problems among patients over the last decade. GM foods might be colonizing the gut flora of North Americans.

12. Elisabeth Kübler-Ross, *On Death and Dying* (New York: Macmillan, 1969).

## Chapter 9: Jesus Was Up Against the Same Thing

1. Our discussion of the Lord's Prayer is based upon Marcus Borg, *The Heart of Christianity: Rediscovering a Life of Faith* (San Francisco: Harper, 2003), 132–37.

2. Richard A. Horsley, *Jesus and Empire: The Kingdom of God and the New World Disorder* (Minneapolis: Fortress, 2003), 21–22.

3. Horsley, *Jesus and Empire*, 9–14, 45, 46, 54; Richard A. Horsley and Neil Asher Silberman, *The Message and the Kingdom* (Minneapolis: Fortress, 1997), 18, 19; Richard A. Horsley, *Jesus and the Spiral of Violence* (Minneapolis: Fortress, 1993), 29–35.

4. Horsley, *Jesus and Empire*, 28–30; Josephus, *Antiquities*, 17.213–18.

5. Horsley, *Jesus and Empire*, 29, 39; Horsley, *The Message and the Kingdom*, 20, 24, 40, 41.

6. Bill Broadway, "'Excavating Jesus': Some Sites Mentioned in Gospels Yield Clues," *Seattle Times* (December 27, 2003).

7. Borg, *Heart of Christianity*, 91–96.

8. Horsley, *Jesus and Empire*, 21–24.

9. Ibid., 25.

10. Borg, *Heart of Christianity*, 91.

11. Ibid., 130.

12. Ibid., 134. Borg writes,

> Forgive us our debts? Or sins? Or trespasses? Part of the reason for uncertainty is different English translations of the gospel texts. But it is also because there are three versions of the Lord's Prayer in early Christianity. Matthew and Luke each have one, as does the *Didache*, an early Christian document written around the year 100.

In wording that is almost identical, Matthew and the *Didache* both have "debt": "And forgive us our *debts*, as we also have forgiven our *debtors*." Luke's version is different. Luke has "sins" in the first half: "And forgive us our sins, for we ourselves forgive everyone indebted to us."

13. Robert Jewett, *Jesus Against the Rapture* (Philadelphia: Westminster Press, 1979), 51–65.

14. Marcus Borg, *Jesus: A New Vision* (San Francisco: Harper, 1987), 96.

15. *The Jerusalem Bible* (Garden City, NY: Doubleday, 1966), 125.

16. Walter Wink, "Toward a Social Psychology of Domination," 2; Wink, "Why Turn the Other Cheek?" *Spirituality and Health* 7:5 (October, 2004): 60. See also Wink, *Engaging the Powers*.

17. Our interpretation of Luke 19:11–27 was originally inspired by James Lockman, OFM, "Re-examining the Parable of the Pounds," unpublished paper, Graduate Theological Union, Berkeley, CA. See also Megan McKenna, *Parables: The Arrows of God* (Maryknoll, NY: Orbis, 1994), 118–21.

## Chapter 10: Healing Our Diminished Sense of Self

1. Joseph Chilton Pearce, interview with Michael Toms, "Adventures of the Mind" (San Francisco: New Dimensions, 1996); personal communication from Michael Mendizza (Dr. Pearce's associate), August 30, 2010.

2. Rupert Sheldrake, *Dogs That Know When Their Owners Are Coming Home and Other Unexplained Powers of Animals* (New York: Three Rivers Press, 1999). A remarkable example of such

powers, in the form of an elephant painting a self-portrait, can be viewed at http://www.youtube.com/watch?v=He7Ge7Sogrk.

3. "Extraordinary Creative and Psychic Powers of Animals," Mercola.com, September 11, 2008, http://articles.mercola.com/sites/articles/archive/2008/09/11/extraordinary-creative-and-psychic-powers-of-animals.aspx (accessed September 6, 2010).

4. Rupert Sheldrake, *The Sense of Being Stared At* (New York: Crown, 2003), 24–27, 300–305; Alex Kirby, "Parrot's Oratory Stuns Scientists," *BBC News Online*, www.animalliberationfront.com/Philosophy/Morality/Speciesism/Nkisi (accessed August 21, 2010).

5. Sheldrake, *Dogs That Know*, 29–63, 70. Dr. Sheldrake included updated statistics in his presentation, "The Unexplained Powers of Animals," at the Science and Consciousness Conference, Santa Fe, NM, 2002.

6. Ibid., 70.

7. Sheldrake, "The Unexplained Powers of Animals."

8. Sheldrake, *The Sense of Being Stared At*, 106–9.

9. Ibid., 95–110; "Rupert Sheldrake Study into Phone Telepathy," www.cnn.com/2006/TECH/science/09/05/telepathy.reut, August 16, 2009; Jay Walljasper, "A Heretic for Our Times," *Ode* 3:9 (November, 2005): 29.

10. Lisa McLaughlin, "In Brief," *Time* (June 26, 2000): 82, http://search.aol.com/aol/search?query=Time&s_it=keyword_rollover (accessed August 30, 2010).

11. Personal communication from Tom Beckman, May 25, 2010, tom.heartmath.com.

12. Childre and Martin, *The HeartMath Solution*, 38.

13. Ibid., 39.

14. Sheldrake, *The Sense of Being Stared At*, 100–101.

15. Larry Dossey, *Healing Words* (San Francisco: Harper, 1993), 49.

16. Ibid., 11011. Dossey quotes researcher F. W. H. Myers: "Love is a kind of exalted but unspecialized telepathy—the simplest and most universal expression of that mutual gravitation or kinship of spirits which is the foundation of the telepathic law."

17. Deepak Chopra, *Grow Younger, Live Longer: Ten Steps to Reverse Aging* (New York: Three Rivers Press, 2002), 47.

18. Rollin McCraty and Dana Tomasino, "Emotional Stress, Positive Emotions and Psychophysiological Coherence," HeartMath Research Center, 2006, http://www.alternativeworldwidehealth.com/files/Heartmath_Stress_chapter.pdf (accessed September 3, 2010).

19. Bill Harris, *Thresholds of the Mind* (Beaverton, OR: Centerpointe Press, 2002), 18. Cited in Judy Cannato, *Field of Compassion* (Notre Dame, IN: Sorin, 2010), 116–17.

20. Chopra, *Grow Younger, Live Longer*, 27–28.

21. Ibid., 19.

22. B. R. Levy, et al., "Longevity Increased by Positive Self-Perceptions of Aging," *Journal of Personality and Social Psychology* 83:2 (August, 2002): 261–70.

23. Harman, "Biology Revisioned," 16–17.

24. Ibid., 17.

25. Owen Barfield, "The Evolution Complex," *Towards* 2:2 (Spring, 1982): 6–16, cited in Harman, "Biology Revisioned," 41.

26. Harman, "Biology Revisioned," 39, 40.

27. Ibid., 12–17, 39–42; Lipton, "Embracing the Immaterial Universe," 8–12; Lipton, *The Biology of Belief*; Rupert Sheldrake, "Memory and Morphic Resonance," presentation at the Science and Consciousness Conference, Santa Fe, NM, April, 2008.

28. Harman, "Biology Revisioned," 16, 39.

29. Pierre Teilhard de Chardin, *The Phenomenon of Man* (New York: Harper & Row, 1965), 151.

30. C. W. F. McClare, "Resonance in Bioenergetics," *Annals of the New York Academy of Science* 227 (1974): 74–97. Cited in

Lipton, *The Biology of Belief*, 81. Lipton writes that McClare's research "revealed that energetic signaling mechanisms such as electromagnetic frequencies are a hundred times more efficient in relaying environmental information than physical signals such as hormones, neurotransmitters, growth factors, etc."

31. Lynne McTaggart, *The Intention Experiment* (New York: Free Press, 2007), xiii.

32. In a controlled experiment measuring the number of cancerous and healthy cells in a culture, Dr. Leonard Laskow demonstrated how intention and the imagination inhibit or promote cellular growth. When he visualized many more cells remaining in the culture, the cancerous cells increased 15 percent. When he imagined fewer cells, the cancerous cells diminished by 20 percent. When he focused his intention on the cells that they return to their healthy state, the cancerous cells decreased by 20 percent, and when this was combined with imagery of fewer cells, there was a 40 percent inhibition of cancerous cells, compared to no change in the number of cancerous cells in the control colonies. This and other experiments show that positive thoughts and images are energy signals that do affect the cells and would contribute to the effectiveness of prayer. Larry Dossey, *Be Careful What You Pray For* (New York: Harper, 1997), 174–75.

33. For a summary of muscle testing, see Robert Blaich, *Your Inner Pharmacy: Taking Back Our Wellness* (Hillsboro, OR: Beyond Words Publishing, 2006), 50–52. Occasionally muscle testing is distorted by a condition known as *psychological reversal*, which can have a variety of causes, including food allergies. See ibid., 150–63.

34. Walter Brown, "The Best Medicine," *Psychology Today* (September, 1997): 58. Regarding Parkinson's disease, see W. Gibbs, "All In the Mind," *Scientific American* (October, 2001): 16. Regarding baldness, see Sandra Blakeslee, "Placebos Prove So

Powerful Even Experts Are Surprised," *New York Times* (October 13, 1998): C-3.

35. Laurie Tarkan, "Fever Phobia and Other Parental Bugaboos," *New York Times* (July 23, 2002): D-4.

36. Margaret Talbot, "The Placebo Prescription," *New York Times Magazine* (January 9, 2001): 34–60.

37. Bruce Lipton, "The Wisdom of Your Cells," audio CD program (Boulder CO: Sounds True, 2006), tape 3. For example, in experiments involving healers, when a healer set an intention toward a subject, the energetic signal of the healer's intention was so powerful that "every last thought appeared to augment or diminish something else's light....When you send an intention, every major physiological system in your body is mirrored in the body of the receiver." McTaggart, *The Intention Experiment,* 46–47.

38. Lipton, "Wisdom of Your Cells."

39. The lottery is called "The Numbers" and is broadcast live on television. Michael Virtanen, "Eerie 9-1-1 Lottery Draws Interest," Associated Press, September 12, 2002; Sue Chan, "Thousands Had Winning 9-1-1 Numbers," http://www.cbsnews.com/stories/2002/09/11/national/main521749.shtml (accessed February 5, 2011).

In 2005, Dr. Bruce Lipton checked the Web site for the New York State Lottery, www.nylottery.org, for the winning numbers on 9/11/02 and sent us the screen capture for that day, which we have. The Web site goes back only five years, and so the same image is no longer available. Personal communication from Dr. Lipton, June 28, 2009.

See also Dean Radin, "For Whom the Bell Tolls," *IONS: Noetic Sciences Review* 63 (March–May, 2003): 11–13, for research on statistically significant deviations in the results of random number generator tests on September 11, 2001. These deviations began about two hours *before* the first plane hit the

World Trade Center, suggesting a widespread, if largely unconscious, premonition. It appears that "a sustained period of very high, worldwide, coherent attention" affected the random number generators.

40. Philip Hallie, *Lest Innocent Blood Be Shed: The Story of the Village of Le Chambon and How Goodness Happened There* (New York: HarperCollins, 1994). See also the documentary film by Pierre Sauvage, who was hidden in Le Chambon as a child, *Weapons of the Spirit* (1989–2007), DVD available from http://www.chambon.org/weapons_en.htm (accessed August 29, 2010).

41. John Hagelin, "Quantum Physical Foundations of Higher States," presentation at the International Science and Consciousness Conference, Albuquerque, NM, 2000; John S. Hagelin et al., "Effects of Group Practice of the Transcendental Meditation Program on Preventing Violent Crime in Washington, D.C.: Results of the National Demonstration Project, June–July, 1993," *Social Indicators Research* 47 (1999): 153–201. See also David Orme-Johnson et al., "International Peace Project in the Middle East: The Effects of the Maharishi Technology of the Unified Field," *Journal of Conflict Resolution* 32:4 (December, 1988): 776–812, for a discussion of the effect of prayer on the relationship between Israel and Lebanon.

42. Mark Mitchell, MFCC, *Sober Times* (San Diego, July, 1988); also cited in Barbara Yoder, *The Recovery Resource Book* (New York: Simon and Schuster, 1990), 65.

## Chapter 11: What About the Chocolate?: Healing the Future by Meeting Our Needs in the Present

1. Dennis Linn and Matthew Linn, *Healing of Memories* (New York/Mahwah, NJ: Paulist Press, 1974).

2. Rosenberg, *Nonviolent Communication: A Language of Compassion*. See also Inbal and Miki Kashtan, "Nonviolent Communication Primer," 2006, http://www.personalgrowthcourses.net/stories/nvc.nonviolent_communication (accessed August 30, 2010). For a wide variety of additional books, articles and audio and video programs, see www.cnvc.org.

3. Although there are four steps in NVC, the key is expressing feelings and needs. Inbal and Miki Kashtan, in their article "Nonviolent Communication Primer," observe that "In an ongoing process of dialogue, there is often no need to mention either the observation (it is usually clear in the context of communication) or the request (since we are already acting on an assumed request for empathy). We might get to guessing a request only after we have connected more and are ready to explore strategies."

A resource for helping children learn to express feelings and needs is the card game "Grok," available from www.nvcproducts.com.

## Chapter 12: Meeting Our Needs Every Day: Sleeping with Bread

1. Dennis Linn, Sheila Fabricant Linn and Matthew Linn, *Sleeping with Bread: Holding What Gives You Life* (New York/Mahwah NJ: Paulist Press, 1995), 1. This book discusses the examen process in detail, including common questions, and would serve as a complement to this chapter.

2. Andrew Cohen, "A Mysterious Urge to Evolve," www.andrewcohen.org/quote/?quote=109 (accessed September 11, 2010).

3. Jack Kornfield, *The Art of Forgiveness, Lovingkindness and Peace* (New York: Bantam, 2002), cited in *Spirituality and Health* (April, 2003): 76. This story is the basis for Dennis Linn, Sheila Fabricant Linn and Matthew Linn, *What Is My Song?* (Mahwah, NJ: Paulist Press, 2005).

The approach of recalling the good things a person has done would need to be modified with those who suffer from personality disorders, such as narcissism or sociopathy. Such people present a false self and may engage in seemingly kind or generous actions for manipulative and self-serving reasons. To recount such actions may be counterproductive, because it may affirm and reinforce the false self and make it all the more difficult to recover the real self. For such people, confrontation may be more healing. See Len Sperry, *Ministry and Community* (Collegeville, MN: Liturgical Press, 2000).

4. See "The Real Secret," by physicist Peter Russell, in *Ode* 5:8 (October, 2007): 74–75, for a discussion of the idea that we can create our own reality through positive thinking.

5. Peter A. Campbell and Edwin M. McMahon, *Bio-Spirituality—Focusing As a Way to Grow*, 2nd ed. (Chicago: Loyola, 1997).

6. Ibid.

7. "What Grown-Ups Understand About Child Development: ZERO TO THREE Survey Results," http://main.zerotothree.org/site/PageServer?pagename=ter_key_childdevt_surveydata&AddInterest=1153 (accessed August 30, 2010).

8. For simple ways to support children in being with their feelings, see Edwin McMahon, "Helping Children Develop the Habit of 'Noticing' and 'Nurturing' Their Important Feelings,"

http://www.biospiritual.org/pages/child-page3.html (accessed August 31, 2010); Linns, *Making Heart-Bread*, "A Note to Parents."

9. Rollin McCraty and Doc Childre, "The Appreciative Heart: The Psychophysiology of Positive Emotions and Optimal Functioning" (Boulder Creek, CA: Institute of HeartMath, 2002), 2, http://thewellbeingconnection.com/AppreciativeHeart7-8-07w_cover_1_.pdf (accessed August 31, 2010).

10. John Taylor Gatto, "Take Back Your Education," *Yes! Magazine* 51 (Fall, 2009): 18.

## Chapter 13: Coming Out from Under the Cloud

1. Steven E. Freeman and Joel Bleifuss, *Was the 2004 Presidential Election Stolen? Exit Polls, Election Fraud and the Official Count* (New York: Seven Stories Press, 2006); Mark Crispin Miller, *Fooled Again* (New York: Basic Books, 2005).

2. Freeman and Bleifuss, *Was the 2004 Presidential Election Stolen?* 58–60; Miller, *Fooled Again*, 32–36. See also www.blackboxvoting.org (accessed February 10, 2011).

3. For at least the past fifty to sixty years, the U.S. government has possessed the technology for new energy generation systems that would eliminate the use of fossil fuels. See Steven Greer, "The Unacknowledged Threat," *Foreign Affairs Journal* 8:2 (April–June, 2004, updated August 18, 2004): 40–57, available from contact/worldaffairsjournal.com and worldaffairs/vsnl.com; Steven Greer, "Implications for the Environment, World Peace, World Poverty and the Human Future," March 2001, http://thebonefly.com/blog/?p=365 (accessed August 30, 2010); "Obama Briefing Documents, March 10, 2010, http://www.disclosureproject.org/docs/obama/index.shtml (accessed September 3, 2010). See also www.disclosureproject.org and www.cseti.org.

This technology comes from extraterrestrial sources that appear to be benevolent, e.g., from the study of downed extraterrestrial vehicles. Strange as this may sound, it is well documented, and the possibility of extraterrestrial contact is being introduced into the mainstream with less ridicule and/or fear mongering than was common in the past. For example, see the recent book by mainstream journalist Leslie Kean, with a foreword by John Podesta (former White House chief of staff), *UFOs: Generals, Pilots and Government Officials Go on the Record* (New York: Crown, 2010). See also a three-minute clip that was broadcast on CNN on September 27, 2010, in which U.S. Air Force officers testified at the National Press Club in Washington, DC, that nuclear missiles were deactivated by UFOs. The moderator representing the officers interprets this to mean that extraterrestrials are trying to warn us of the danger of nuclear weapons. http://www.cnn.com/video/#/video/us/2010/09/27/bts.ufo.activity.cnn (accessed February 5, 2011). The testimony of these officers was also covered by many other mainstream news organizations, including ABC News, September 27, 2010, http://abcnews.go.com/Technology/airmen-govt-clean-ufos/story?id=11738715 (accessed February 10, 2011), and CBS News, September 27, 2010, http://www.cbsnews.com/stories/2010/09/28/national/main6907702.shtml (accessed February 10, 2011).

4. For an overview of the deceptions behind U.S. wars, see Howard Zinn, *A People's History of the United States* (New York: HarperCollins, 2005).

5. In his memoir, *The Age of Turbulence: Adventures in a New World* (New York: Penguin, 2007), Alan Greenspan writes, "I am saddened that it is politically inconvenient to acknowledge what everyone knows: the Iraq war is largely about oil." Cited in Peter Beaumont and Joanna Walters, "Greenspan Admits Iraq War Was About Oil, as Deaths Put at 1.2m," *The Observer* (September 16, 2007). Regarding Paul Wolfowitz, see George Wright, "Wolfowitz: Iraq War Was about Oil," *The Guardian* (June 4, 2003).

6. Unfortunately, Eisenhower's policies contributed to American militarism in ways that belie the beauty of these words. See Ira Chernus, "How One Paragraph in a Single Speech Has Skewed the Eisenhower Record," January 19, 2011, http://truth-out.org/print/66953 (accessed January 19, 2011), and David Swanson, "What Eisenhower Got Wrong," *Global Research*, January 13, 2011, http://www.globalresearch.ca/PrintArticle.php?articleId=22776 (accessed January 18, 2011).

7. Andreas, *Addicted to War*, 44; Michael Renner, *National Security: The Economic and Environmental Dimensions* (Washington, DC: World Watch Institute, 1989), 23.

8. Lawrence S. Wittner, "A Nation That Spends More Money on War Than Life Is Approaching Spiritual Death," www.buzzflash.com, August 16, 2010 (accessed August 17, 2010). Dr. King's actual words were, "A nation that continues year after year to spend more money on military defense than on programs of social uplift is approaching spiritual death."

9. Joan Chittister, "How Shall We Live?" *Spirituality and Health* (December, 2003): 28–33.

10. According to UNICEF, approximately three billion people live on less than $2.00 per day, and 1.4 billion of those live on less than $1.25 per day. http://internationalpeaceandconflict.org/video/one-days-wages-odw-is-a?xg_source=activity (accessed August 14, 2010).

11. David Bromwich, "America's Wars: How Serial War Became the American Way of Life," tomdispatch.com, July 22, 2009, http://www.huffingtonpost.com/david-bromwich/americas-wars-how-serial_b_242347.html (accessed September 5, 2010).

12. Kübler-Ross, *On Death and Dying*; Linns, *Healing Life's Hurts*.

## Chapter 14: The Healing Power of the Small

1. David Steindl-Rast, OSB, from his Web site, www.gratefulness.org This quote may be found at http://www.gratefulness.org/qbox/item.cfm?qbox_id:135: (accessed February 11, 2011).

2. Walter Wink, "Why Turn the Other Cheek?" *Spirituality and Health* 7:5 (October, 2004): 63.

3. Angie O'Gorman, ed., *The Universe Bends Toward Justice* (Philadelphia: New Society Publishers, 1990), 241–47.

4. Stephen Zunes writes:

> The power of nonviolent action has been acknowledged even by such groups as Freedom House, a Washington-based organization with close ties to the foreign policy establishment. Its 2005 study observed that of the nearly 70 countries that have made the transition from dictatorship to varying degrees of democracy in the past 30 years, only a small minority did so through armed struggle from below or reform instigated from above. Hardly any new democracies resulted from foreign invasion. In nearly three-quarters of the transitions, change was rooted in democratic civil-society organizations that employed nonviolent methods. In addition, the study noted that countries where nonviolent civil resistance movements played a major role tend to have freer and more stable democratic systems.

A different study, published last year in the journal *International Security*, used an expanded database and analyzed 323 major insurrections in support of self-determination and democratic rule since 1900. It found that violent resistance was successful only 26 percent of the time, whereas nonviolent campaigns had a 53 percent success rate ("Weapons of Mass Democracy," *Yes! Magazine* 51 [September 22, 2009]: 53).

5. Ronald Rolheiser, *Holy Longing* (New York: Doubleday, 1999), 189.
6. Walter Wink, "The Redeeming Power of the Small," *Fellowship* 66:1–2 (January–February, 2000): 4.
7. Jane Marks, *The Hidden Children: The Secret Survivors of the Holocaust* (New York: Fawcett Columbine, 1993), 206–7.
8. Zinn, "The Optimism of Uncertainity."

# RESOURCES FOR FURTHER GROWTH

## Books and Audiovisual Materials

The Linns are the authors of twenty-two books, including *Sleeping with Bread: Holding What Gives You Life, Healing of Memories, Healing Life's Hurts, Good Goats: Healing Our Image of God* and *Healing the Eight Stages of Life*. Their books for children include *What Is My Song?* and *Making Heart-Bread.* These books and others by the authors are available from Paulist Press, 997 Macarthur Blvd., Mahwah, NJ 07430; phone orders: (800) 218-1903; fax orders: (800) 836-3161; Web site: www.paulistpress.com.

All of the Linns' books and audiovisual materials, as well as courses, are available from: Christian Video Library, 3914-A Michigan Ave., St. Louis MO 63118; phone (314) 865-0729; fax (314) 773-3115. DVDs may be borrowed on a donation basis.

These materials are listed on the Linns' Web site, www.linnministries.org.

## Spanish Books and Tapes

All of the Linns' books and most of their CDs and DVDs are available in Spanish. For more information, please contact Christian Video Library or see their Web site, www.linnministries.org.

## Retreats and Conferences

For information about retreats and conferences by the authors, please call (970) 476-9235 or see their Web site, www.linnministries.org.

# ABOUT THE AUTHORS

Dennis, Sheila and Matt Linn give retreats and seminars on processes for healing and reconciliation that integrate spirituality with psychology, medicine and science. They have worked in over sixty countries and in many universities and hospitals, and have given a course for doctors accredited by the American Medical Association. Dennis and Matt are coauthors of twenty-two books, the last seventeen coauthored with Sheila. These books have sold over a million copies in English and have been translated into more than twenty languages. Dennis and Sheila live in Colorado with their son, John, whom they are home- and global-schooling. Matt lives in a Jesuit community in Minnesota.

Their purpose is to support personal growth and the evolution of our planet by integrating spirituality, psychology and science in ways that empower all of us to heal personal and social wounds and discover our unique gifts for carrying out the special purpose of our lives. Their ministry is committed to the nonviolent resolution of personal and social conflicts, care for the earth, gender and racial equality, economic justice and respect for all faith traditions. Their roots are in Ignatian spirituality, which emphasizes finding the presence of the mystery we call God in all things.